UNITED TASTES OF
TEXAS

Southern Living®

UNITED TASTES OF
TEXAS

AUTHENTIC RECIPES FROM ALL CORNERS OF THE LONE STAR STATE

★★★ JESSICA DUPUY ★★★

Oxmoor
House®

INTRODUCTION

As a fourth generation Texan, my experience with cooking began when I was two years old, sitting on the kitchen counter watching my mother make chicken 'n' dumplings or peppered steak or maybe gumbo from the wild ducks my father hunted along the rice fields near Houston. Gumbo aside, her specialty was baking. She could add a few tweaks to the average store-bought chocolate cake mix that would wow the ladies at our community church bake sales.

But home cooking didn't begin with just my mother. It was the language of our family. Every weekend gathering or holiday get-together revolved around one conversation: What are we eating, and who is bringing what? Between my grandmother, my three aunts, and now my six cousins and their extended families, our gatherings are often a showcase of new recipes collected from myriad local Junior League cookbooks, community recipe exchanges and cooking magazines. Our favorite types of recipes? The ones that remind us of home: Texas.

While Texas is a western extension of the Deep South, our culinary history reflects the influences of far-flung, international cultures. The "Six Flags Over Texas" are often referred to as the state's primary cultural influences relating to the six different countries that have had sovereignty over some or all of the current territory since 1519 including Spain, France, Mexico, The Republic of Texas, The Confederate States of America and the United States of America. These cultures have intermingled over five centuries to create distinct styles of food. Many other cultures have also left their mark, from German, Czech, and African-American, to Irish, New Mexican, and Native American. The roots of these flavors include everything from piquant Latin American spices to slow-cooked meats laced with layers of wood-burned smoke, and a smattering of bright, citrus-kissed seafood caught fresh from the Gulf Coast.

To understand Texas food is to understand its regional diversity. Ribeye steaks represent the Panhandle, while Tex-Mex flourishes in the Valley and up through San Antonio. Czech kolaches are found north of Austin and soulful German sausages grace the Hill Country. Savory fried seafood and boiled shrimp are highlights from the coast, just like fried chicken in East Texas and West Texas chili. Combined, these are the flavors that are uniquely Texan.

Most days, I cook at home as a way to spend time with my five-year-old son, Gus—who is named after Texas Ranger Augustus McCrae from the iconic Texas historical fiction novel, *Lonesome Dove*. It's not just about the time we spend together; it's about giving him a sense of identity. If the food we grow up with is a piece of who we are, then Gus, like myself and many other Texans, will no doubt know his roots are planted deep in the Lone Star State.

— Jessica Dupuy

Published by Oxmoor House, an imprint of Time Inc. Books
225 Liberty Street, New York, NY 10281

Writer: Jessica Dupuy
Senior Editor: Katherine Cobbs
Editor: Sarah A. Gleim
Assistant Project Editor: Lacie Pinyan
Art Director: Christopher Rhoads
Designer: Julie Savasky
Executive Photography Director: Iain Bagwell
Photo Editor: Kellie Lindsey
Senior Photographer: Hélène Dujardin
Photographers: Kenny Braun, Jody Horton, Wyatt McSpadden,
      Gustav Schmiege III
Senior Photo Stylists: Kay E. Clarke, Mindi Shapiro Levine
Food Stylists: Nathan Carrabba, Victoria E. Cox,
      Margaret Monroe Dickey, Catherine Crowell Steele
Test Kitchen Manager: Alyson Moreland Haynes
Senior Recipe Developer and Tester: Callie Nash
Recipe Developers and Testers: Julia Levy, Karen Rankin
Assistant Production Manager: Diane Rose Keener
Assistant Production Director: Sue Chodakiewicz
Copy Editors: Donna Baldone, Ashley Strickland Freeman
Proofreader: Julie Bosché
Illustrator: Steven Noble
Indexer: Mary Ann Laurens
Fellows: Jessica Baude, Dree Deacon, Rishon Hanners,
      Olivia Pierce, Natalie Schumann, Mallory Short, Abigail Wilt

ISBN-13: 978-0-8487-4580-6

Library of Congress Control Number: 2016941187

Printed in the United States of America

10 9 8 7 6 5 4 3

CONTENTS

CHAPTER ONE

CENTRAL ★ TEXAS ★

A region showcased for its idyllic hilly landscape, Central Texas owes much of its culinary heritage to German and Czech immigrants who settled here in the 1800s. The Germans settled areas such as New Braunfels and Fredericksburg, and the Czechs from northeastern Bohemia to the Blackland Prairie areas between Austin and Houston. Cattle and agriculture became the primary commerce, and both cultures gave rise to a distinctive style of smoking meat that defines Texas barbecue today.

BACON-WRAPPED DOVE POPPERS

Growing up in a hunting family, dove season was almost as important as the opening day of football season. On a good hunt, I would always look forward to this special snack. The cream cheese tones down the spicy jalapeño. If you don't have dove around, use chunks of pork or beef as a substitute. (Chicken gets too dry.) You may cut the bacon slices in half if you prefer.

Makes *8 to 10 servings* · **Hands-on** *30 min.* · **Total** *50 min., not including rub*

30 skinned and boned dove breasts
Texas Meat Rub (see sidebar)
1 (8-oz.) package cream cheese, softened
4 jalapeño peppers*, seeded and cut into
   30 thin strips

2 (16-oz.) packages bacon slices
Wooden picks

1. Preheat grill to 350° to 400°F (medium-high) heat. Sprinkle dove with Texas Meat Rub. Spoon 2 tsp. cream cheese, and place 1 jalapeño slice on 1 side of each dove breast, leaving a ¼-inch border. Roll up starting at 1 short side. Wrap each stuffed jalapeño with 1 bacon slice; secure with wooden picks.
2. Grill dove, uncovered, 6 minutes on each side or until bacon is crisp and dove is done.

*Serrano peppers or red Fresno peppers may be substituted for jalapeño peppers.

Texas Meat Rub

Stir together ¼ cup table salt, ¼ cup ancho chile powder, ¼ cup garlic powder, ¼ cup onion powder, ¼ cup seasoned salt, ¼ cup freshly ground black pepper, and 2 Tbsp. paprika until well blended. Store in an airtight container up to 1 year.
Makes *1 ²/₃ cup*

HILL COUNTRY POTATO SALAD

In Central Texas, you'll find potato salad usually one of two ways. One is as a mayonnaise-dressed mixture of potato, onion, and often dill to serve alongside barbecue. The other is vinegar- or mustard-based German-style potato salad served with traditional German fare in towns like Fredericksburg and New Braunfels. While this prized family version has quite a few more ingredients than the German standard, it's similar in that it's best served warm. If you like pickles in your potato salad, try Best Maid or Del-Dixi dill pickles from Fort Worth.

Makes *8 to 10 servings* · **Hands-on** *30 min.* · **Total** *45 min.*

2 ½ lb. medium-size baby Yukon gold
   potatoes
2 tsp. table salt
6 center-cut bacon slices
4 large hard-cooked eggs, peeled and diced
¾ cup chopped celery

½ cup chopped green onions
¼ cup chopped fresh parsley
1 (4-oz.) jar diced pimiento, drained
2 Tbsp. coarse-grained mustard
½ cup diced dill pickles (optional)

1. Bring potatoes, salt, and water to cover to a boil in a medium saucepan over medium-high heat. Reduce heat to medium-low, and cook 10 to 15 minutes or until tender; drain and rinse under cold water 1 minute. Drain well.
2. Cook bacon in a large skillet over medium-low heat 8 minutes or until crisp; remove bacon, and drain on paper towels, reserving 2 Tbsp. drippings. Crumble bacon.
3. Peel potatoes, and cut into 1-inch pieces. Combine potatoes, bacon, reserved 2 Tbsp. warm drippings, eggs, next 5 ingredients, and pickles, if desired, in a large bowl. Add salt and black pepper to taste. Serve warm or at room temperature.

LA BARBECUE CHARRO BEANS

Charro or barbecue beans are a common fixture with both barbecue and Tex-Mex cuisines. Most people can take them or leave them, but I like it when a restaurant finds a way to make their beans memorable. La Barbecue, a simple food trailer on the east side of Austin, churns out some of the best barbecue in town. Though their peppery brisket is what's most coveted, they make sure to serve memorable side dishes as well. The addition of fresh cilantro lends a bright flavor to these beans.

Makes *8 to 10 servings* · **Hands-on** *20 min.* · **Total** *5 hours, 20 min., plus soaking time*

1 (16-oz.) package dried pinto beans
1 yellow onion, chopped
$^1/_2$ cup canned crushed tomatoes
1 jalapeño pepper, seeded and chopped
$^3/_4$ lb. salt pork

1 Tbsp. chili powder
2 tsp. ground cumin
1 $^1/_2$ tsp. freshly ground black pepper
1 tsp. garlic powder
$^1/_2$ cup chopped fresh cilantro

1. Place pinto beans in a Dutch oven. Cover with cold water 2 inches above beans; cover and let soak 8 hours.
2. Drain beans; transfer to a Dutch oven. Add onion, next 7 ingredients, and water to cover 1 $^1/_2$ inches above beans. Bring to a boil; cover, reduce heat, and simmer 1 hour, stirring occasionally. Partially uncover pot, and simmer 2 $^1/_2$ hours.
3. Remove lid, and simmer 1 hour, stirring occasionally. Stir in cilantro, and simmer 20 to 30 minutes or until beans are tender. Add salt and pepper to taste.

TEXAS TOOLS

Cazuela

Though often referred to us beans, stew, or soup, the term cazuela is actually the vessel in which the meal is cooked. In South Texas it is often simply referred to as a "bean pot."

ANDREW WISEHEART

CHEF/OWNER CONTIGO AND GARDNER, AUSTIN

A wanderer. A traveler. A chef. Andrew Wiseheart isn't your ordinary kitchen crusader. He's got all of the skills and techniques of a classically trained chef rolled up in the back pocket of his dusty pair of jeans. But he's also got a solid foundation of hard work and Texas ranch simplicity that ground him to the soles of his worn leather boots. He's a man at home goat-roping in the western stretches of Central Texas, bivouacking around the backroads of Eastern Europe, or whipping up a classic béchamel sauce in a Michelin-rated Napa Valley kitchen.

Originally from San Angelo, a town that roughly serves as a gateway from the Hill Country to West Texas, Wiseheart grew up in a place built on cotton farming and cattle and goat ranching. For him, the two driving forces in life have always been land and food. And it's the people and culture from both of these elements that have guided him along.

During a ten-year chapter of his life, he spent roughly every 16 months in a different state or country following high school. In a progression from college to culinary school to alternating years in the Napa Valley kitchens of Brix, La Toque, and Angele and personal excursions to villages in Italy, Croatia, Slovenia, and other European countries, the year he spent working at a restaurant in Italy probably afforded him the most impact.

"It was such an old-world experience to be in those different places," says Wiseheart. "There were olive orchards and vineyards everywhere. Everyone had gardens and provided for themselves. Every place really had similar approaches to their food—they just had different ingredients to work with. That's when I realized there was really no reason I couldn't be doing the same thing back in Texas."

He worked as a line cook in Austin at several different restaurants before opening Contigo with business partner Ben Edgerton in May 2011 on the east side of town near the city's old airport. The patio-centric establishment drew national acclaim serving rustic Texas fare with everything from ox tongue sliders with pickled green tomato and creamy cauliflower gratin to roasted chicken and fingerling potatoes with capers and rabbit and sage dumplings.

"Charcuterie fits so well here as something to eat when you're sitting outdoors. Same with grilled and smoked meats," says Wiseheart. "We pull it together with whatever vegetables are in season and all of a sudden, you're eating something that fits with the time of year and specific place."

In 2014, they opened Gardner, named for Wiseheart's father, and an elegant, citified answer to Contigo's rustic, country vibe. While he keeps his hands full with managing the kitchen needs of two restaurants, he still makes time to head back home to San Angelo a couple of times a year for ranch work.

"Once you get outside of the city, here life is much slower. That's what I love about it," says Wiseheart. "I still work cows and goats because that's what I love. Your day starts on the front porch when the sun comes up and ends on the porch when the sun goes down. Between those times you get out there with the guys and work a hard day. They're my fellowship and that's my church. It reminds me that the people and the land from which you come will always be the most important."

RABBIT AND SAGE DUMPLINGS

A nod to the German lineage of the region, this is one of Chef Andrew Wiseheart's signature dishes at his Austin restaurant, Contigo.

Makes *6 to 8 servings* · **Hands-on** *1 hour, 50 min.* · **Total** *3 hours, 40 min.*

SAGE DUMPLINGS
3 cups all-purpose flour
3 tsp. baking powder
1 tsp. table salt
$^3/_4$ tsp. baking soda
4 $^1/_2$ Tbsp. cold butter, cut into pieces
1 $^1/_2$ cups buttermilk
1 $^1/_2$ Tbsp. chopped fresh sage

RABBIT
1 (2 $^3/_4$-lb.) rabbit, cut into 6 pieces
Kosher salt
1 Tbsp. canola oil

2 Tbsp. butter
7 onions, divided
5 carrots, divided
3 celery ribs, cut into 1-inch pieces
5 garlic cloves
3 Tbsp. whole grain mustard, divided
1 (750-ml.) bottle dry white wine
4 to 6 cups chicken broth

$^1/_3$ cup all-purpose flour
1 tsp. table salt, divided
$^1/_2$ tsp. freshly ground black pepper
1 Tbsp. olive oil

1. Prepare Dumplings: Stir together flour and next 3 ingredients in a large bowl; cut in butter with a pastry blender or 2 forks until crumbly. Add buttermilk and sage, stirring just until dry ingredients are moistened. (Do not overmix.)
2. Turn dough out onto a floured surface. Roll to $^3/_4$-inch thickness; cut into 28 (1-inch) pieces. Cover with a damp towel to prevent drying out.
3. Prepare Rabbit: Preheat oven to 300°F. Season rabbit with salt. Cook in hot canola oil in a large skillet over medium heat 2 to 3 minutes. Add butter; cook 3 to 4 minutes. Turn and cook 8 minutes or until golden brown. Transfer to a baking dish, reserving drippings in skillet.
4. Cut 1 onion into 8 wedges; cut 2 carrots into 1-inch pieces. Sauté onion, carrots, celery, and garlic in drippings over medium-high heat 5 minutes. Stir in 2 Tbsp. mustard; cook 3 minutes. Spoon over rabbit.
5. Add wine; simmer until reduced by three-fourths. Pour over rabbit. Add broth to cover. Bake, covered, for 1 hour. Remove and let stand until cool enough to touch. Skin, bone, and shred rabbit, discarding skin and bones. Set aside. Increase oven temperature to 400°F.
6. Strain broth into a saucepan; discard solids. Bring to a simmer over medium heat.
7. Whisk together flour and 3 Tbsp. water to form a paste. Whisk into simmering broth. Cook 3 minutes, whisking constantly. Whisk in $^1/_2$ tsp. salt, pepper, and remaining 1 Tbsp. mustard. Cover and keep warm over low heat.
8. Cut remaining onions into 6 wedges each; dice remaining carrots. Sauté vegetables in olive oil in a cast-iron skillet over medium-high heat 6 minutes or until crisp-tender. Stir in rabbit, broth, and remaining $^1/_2$ tsp. salt. Top with dumplings, about $^1/_2$ inch apart.
9. Bake at 400°F for 20 to 25 minutes or until bubbling and dumplings are done.

TEXAS PIT STOPS

BLUE BONNET CAFE
Marble Falls

FONDA SAN MIGUEL
Austin

HIGH'S CAFE & STORE
Comfort

MONUMENT CAFE
Georgetown

UCHI
Austin

VAUDEVILLE
Fredericksburg

VILLAGE BAKERY
West

SMOKED CHICKEN CORN CHOWDER

Corn is one of my favorite ingredients. Its natural sweetness and versatility add flavor to just about anything. I usually have corn on hand, whether fresh in the summertime or frozen during the winter. This chowder is great for either season, and the smoked chicken is a perfect complement. For a twist, substitute grilled shrimp for the smoked chicken, and for more of a kick, leave the seeds in the jalapeño.

Makes *6 to 8 servings* · **Hands-on** *35 min.* · **Total** *1 hour*

2 ears fresh corn, husks removed
2 center-cut bacon slices
1 medium onion, chopped
1 (4-oz.) can diced green chiles
1 jalapeño pepper, seeded and chopped
1 chipotle chile pepper in adobo sauce, finely chopped
2 garlic cloves, minced
2 medium-size baking potatoes, peeled and diced

4 cups chicken broth
3 cups shredded Smoked Chicken (page 223)
2 cups heavy cream
3 plum tomatoes, seeded and chopped
1 Tbsp. finely chopped fresh parsley
1 1/2 cups shredded Monterey Jack cheese

1. Cut kernels from cobs. Reserve corn and cobs.
2. Cook bacon in a Dutch oven over medium-low heat 8 minutes or until crisp; remove bacon, and drain on paper towels, reserving drippings in Dutch oven. Crumble bacon.
3. Increase heat to medium-high. Sauté onion and next 4 ingredients in hot drippings 5 minutes or until tender. Add potato, and sauté 1 minute. Add broth and reserved corn cobs, and cook 12 to 15 minutes or until potatoes are tender. Stir in chicken, next 3 ingredients, and corn kernels. Reduce heat to low and simmer, stirring often, 15 minutes or until slightly thickened.
4. Remove from heat. Discard corn cobs. Stir in 1 cup cheese. Ladle into bowls, and sprinkle with remaining 1/2 cup cheese and crumbled bacon.

TEXAS BARBECUE

Perhaps the best explanation of Texas barbecue I've encountered is from noted Texas barbecue expert Daniel Vaughn, whose book, *The Prophets of Smoked Meat,* is an engaging love affair with Texas barbecue culture that catalogs about 500 Texas barbecue joints. According to Vaughn, "Texas barbecue is defined more by what it isn't than what it is." From the wood and rub to the use of sauce or utensils, you'll get an earful all over the state about the way it shouldn't be. Opinions of what exactly it should be are as vast as a Texas blue sky.

EAST TEXAS—THE SOUTHERN BELT
Barbecue here is influenced by settlers and slaves from Louisiana, Arkansas, Tennessee, Georgia, Alabama, and the Carolinas. East Texas 'cue includes quite a bit of pork, although beef has a definite place, primarily in the form of chopped beef brisket and fall-off-the-bone beef ribs. Hot links, a kind of all-beef sausage from the small town of Pittsburg, are one of the region's unique contributions to Texas barbecue, and the sauce here is thick and sweet and always accompanies the meat.

CENTRAL TEXAS—THE DIVIDE
As you move down toward Central Texas, barbecue takes a significant turn. Lockhart, the "Barbecue Capital of Texas," is the epicenter of this style where sauce gives way to dry rubs. In places east of Austin along I-35, restaurants often refuse to serve sauce. Kreuz's Barbecue sells T-shirts touting "No Sauce" and doesn't provide forks for diners. With the German and Czech settlers came old world-style smoked sausages, now an integral piece of the region's barbecue puzzle. It's the all-hallowed smoky beef brisket simply rubbed with salt and pepper and smoked indirectly over oak for hours that reigns. Pork spare ribs are more often trumped by gargantuan hunks of toothsome smoked beef ribs.

HILL COUNTRY MEETS WEST TEXAS
West of Austin, into the Hill Country towns of Llano, Mason, San Angelo, and Brady, another progressive shift occurs. Continued German and Czech influence means beef and sausage play a role, but rather than smoking meats over indirect heat, you see barbecue joints using direct heat methods—a carryover from the campfire cooking of ranchers and cowboys. Here, sauce is acceptable, though it tends to be vinegary and thin. With its rich history of sheep and goat farming, you'll find mutton, lamb, and cabrito (Spanish for baby goat) on the menu.

SOUTH TEXAS BARBACOA
Here, Tex-Mex cookery and barbecue collide, and the resourcefulness of Mexican cooking is celebrated, particularly when it comes to using as much of an animal as possible. Beef continues to star—though pork and goat are also well represented—and wood fire is the primary source of heat. But that's where the similarities end. Here, you find less brisket and more cow head. Cooked overnight to yield rich, silky meat, everything including the cheek, eyes, and tongue are served individually. The corn tortilla serves as the primary vehicle getting food to the mouth, and salsa trumps barbecue sauce as the preferred condiment.

DEBATE

SAUCE OR NO SAUCE

Despite what the meat lovers in Lockhart say, we're at a crossroads: Should you savor your smoked meat dressed with sauce, or eat it like a purist: naked? Sauce makes mediocre 'cue palatable. But even on the best barbecue around, sauce cuts the fattiness of the meat and adds a brightness and dimension. Does good 'cue need it? Nope. But delicious sauce takes great barbecue to a whole 'nother level.

THE MEATS

Meat options on the Texas barbecue menu are as expansive as the Lone Star State itself. Brisket reigns, but beef ribs, hot link sausages, and smoked poultry have a prominent place throughout Central Texas. In East Texas pork figures prominently, while in West Texas beef in all its forms—head, tongue, and jowls—along with sheep and goat are the celebrated offerings.

PULLED PORK
Influenced by its Deep South neighbors, this bit of the pig reigns in East Texas.

BRISKET
Sliced or chopped, sauce or no, the key to success is all in the cooking—low and slow is a must to develop a flavorful bark.

SAUSAGE
Czech and German influence made hot links a barbecue staple in the center of the state.

BEEF RIBS
Almost exclusive to the state, natives prize this big, meaty cut on barbecue plates.

SMOKED CHICKEN OR TURKEY
Domestic or wild, Texans like their birds better bathed in hardwood smoke.

BEANS AND COLESLAW
Sweet-and-savory baked beans and tangy slaw are just a few side-dish standards.

THE SIDES

EXTRAS
Garnishes such as sliced raw onion, bread-and-butter pickles, and hot pickled okra serve as flavor enhancers and palate cleansers.

POTATO SALAD
The potatoes for the favored German-style potato salad might be smoked, but are never dressed with mayonnaise.

THE SAUCE
If sauce is served at all, its tomato-and-brown sugar sweetness is tempered by a healthy dose of vinegar.

SMOKED BRISKET

Throwing around opinions about smoked brisket in Central Texas is a daring endeavor, especially when it comes to the best way to smoke it, the best wood to use, the type of smoker you should use, and whether or not it should have a dry rub as well as a sauce. Among the brisket kings of Central Texas—which include Louie Mueller, Kreuz, Smitty's, Snow's, La Barbecue, and the James Beard Award-winning Franklin Barbecue—a simple rub is key.

Makes *2 to 3 dozen servings* · **Hands-on** *1 hour* · **Total** *24 hours, 40 min.*

Brisket Rub

Stir together ⅓ cup grated piloncillo (or dark brown sugar), 2 ½ Tbsp. kosher salt, 2 ½ Tbsp. seasoned salt, 4 tsp. garlic powder, 4 tsp. ancho chile powder, 2 tsp. freshly ground black pepper, 2 tsp. chile powder, 2 tsp. Texas Meat Rub (page 13), and ¾ tsp. ground cumin until well blended. Store in an airtight container up to 1 month.
Makes *1 cup*

BRISKET BRINE
1 (12-oz.) bottle beer
¼ cup sugar
¼ cup kosher salt
¼ cup seasoned salt
2 Tbsp. garlic powder
2 Tbsp. Texas Meat Rub (page 13)

1 tsp. freshly ground black pepper

1 (14-lb.) beef brisket, trimmed
Brisket Rub (see sidebar)
4 to 5 lb. charcoal briquettes
10 to 12 (20-inch) post oak logs

1. Prepare Brisket Brine: Stir together first 7 ingredients and 8 cups water until salts dissolve. (Refrigerate in an airtight container up to 1 week.) Combine brisket and Brisket Brine. Cover and chill 12 hours.
2. Remove brisket from brine, discarding brine, and rinse well. Coat brisket with Brisket Rub, and let stand 1 hour.
3. Meanwhile, prepare charcoal in an offset smoker according to manufacturer's instructions. Place 3 to 5 logs in a cone-shaped teepee over coals. Maintain internal temperature at 225° to 250°F for 15 to 20 minutes.
4. Place brisket, fat side up, on top grate with pointed, fatty end toward the firebox. Smoke brisket, covered with lid, 8 to 10 hours or until a meat thermometer inserted in center of brisket (where the point and flat meet) registers 175° to 180°F. Maintain temperature inside smoker between 200° and 225°F. Remove brisket, and wrap tightly in aluminum foil. Return brisket to smoker, and smoke 3 to 5 more hours or until thermometer inserted in brisket registers 195° to 200°F. (Check temperature each hour.)
5. Remove brisket from smoker; open foil, and let stand 2 to 4 minutes or until no longer steaming. Let brisket stand, loosely covered with foil, 20 to 30 minutes.
6. Remove brisket from foil, and place on a cutting board. Slice meat across the grain into ⅛- to ¼-inch slices. Serve immediately.

SMOKED BARBECUE BABY BACK RIBS

Though Texas has put its mark on beef barbecue, there has always been room for pork too. For these ribs, start with a dry rub and smoke them for a while. Then baste them with sauce and finish grilling over direct heat to give them a glaze. The key is to get the meat to the point that it's really tender but not completely falling off the bone. Be sure to use a water pan to keep the temperature steady at 225° to 250°F.

Makes *8 servings* · **Hands-on** *15 min.* · **Total** *6 hours, including rub and sauce*

4 slabs baby back pork ribs (about 5 lb.)
Barbecue Rub (see sidebar)
3 to 4 oak, hickory, or pecan wood chunks

BARBECUE SAUCE
1 cup thick barbecue sauce
$1/2$ cup molasses (not blackstrap)
2 canned chipotle peppers in adobo sauce, chopped

1. Rinse and pat ribs dry. If desired, remove thin membrane from back of ribs by slicing into it with a knife and then pulling it off. (This will make ribs more tender.)
2. Coat ribs with Barbecue Rub, and let stand 30 minutes.
3. Soak wood chunks in water 30 minutes.
4. Meanwhile, prepare charcoal fire in smoker according to manufacturer's instructions. Place water pan in smoker; add water to depth of fill line. Regulate temperature with a thermometer at 225° to 250°F for 15 to 20 minutes.
5. Drain wood chunks, and place on coals. Place ribs, bone side up, on upper food grate; close smoker. Smoke ribs 3 hours or until a meat thermometer inserted into thickest portion registers 180° to 185°F. Maintain temperature inside smoker between 225° and 250°F.
6. Prepare Barbecue Sauce: Stir together all ingredients in a small saucepan over medium heat; bring to a boil, reduce heat, and simmer 10 minutes, stirring occasionally.
7. Remove ribs from smoker, and baste both sides with Barbecue Sauce. Wrap ribs tightly in a double layer of heavy-duty aluminum foil, and return to smoker. Cook, bone side down, $1 1/2$ more hours.
8. Remove ribs from smoker; let stand 10 to 15 minutes. Open foil, and allow steam to escape for 2 to 4 minutes. Drain and discard liquid and aluminum foil. Cut between bones to separate ribs, and serve immediately.

Note: For a faster method, prepare as directed through Step 6. Preheat grill to 350° to 400°F (medium-high) heat. Remove ribs from smoker, and baste with Barbecue Sauce. Grill, bone sides down, covered with grill lid, 7 to 8 minutes on each side or until sauce sets. Remove and let stand 10 to 15 minutes. Cut to separate ribs and serve.

Barbecue Rub

Stir together $1/3$ cup grated piloncillo (or dark brown sugar), $2 1/2$ Tbsp. kosher salt, $2 1/2$ Tbsp. seasoned salt, 4 tsp. garlic powder, 4 tsp. ancho chile powder, 2 tsp. freshly ground black pepper, 2 tsp. chile powder, 2 tsp. Texas Meat Rub (page 13), and $3/4$ tsp. ground cumin until well blended. Store in an airtight container up to 1 month.
Makes *1 cup*

TARTE FLAMBÉE

Just west of San Antonio, the small town of Castroville is known as "little Alsace" for its wave of Alsatian immigrants who arrived in the mid 1840s. Alsace is that little sliver of land along the Rhine River between Germany and France whose identity has endured a great many transitions in its history. Partly French and partly German, Alsatian culture is richly layered with both French and German culinary influences. This classic Tarte Flambée is a simple alternative to your everyday pizza.

Makes *6 servings* · **Hands-on** *30 min.* · **Total** *40 min.*

6 bacon slices, diced
1 Tbsp. butter
1 medium onion, thinly sliced
4 oz. crème fraîche (about $^1/_2$ cup)
$^1/_4$ tsp. table salt

$^1/_4$ tsp. freshly ground black pepper
$^1/_8$ tsp. freshly grated nutmeg
1 (12.7-oz.) package prebaked thin
    pizza crust

1. Preheat oven to 450°F. Cook bacon in a medium skillet over medium-high heat 5 minutes or until crisp; remove bacon, and drain on paper towels. Wipe skillet clean.
2. Melt butter in skillet over medium heat; add onion, and sauté 15 minutes or until onion is lightly browned. Remove from heat.
3. Place a baking sheet in oven 5 minutes.
4. Meanwhile, stir together crème fraîche and next 3 ingredients. Spread mixture over pizza crust, leaving a 1-inch border; top with onions and bacon. Transfer pizza onto hot baking sheet.
5. Bake at 450°F for 10 minutes or until edges are golden brown and crisp and topping is bubbly. Remove from oven, and cut into squares. Serve immediately.

JESSE GRIFFITHS

CHEF/OWNER DAI DUE, AUSTIN

Jesse Griffiths runs a full-scale restaurant and butcher shop, but the inspiration for everything he does is from the field, whether from a coursing stream during a morning mayfly hatch, a cactus-covered quail covey terrain, the shoreline at a fading tide, or the ashen pine forests of East Texas in pursuit of morels. Griffiths not only talks about sourcing responsibly and being a committed steward of the land, but he also toes the line.

Originally from Denton, Griffiths got into the restaurant business in high school before making his way to Austin in the '90s where he spent a decade working in the kitchens of notable restaurants Tocai, Jean Luc's Bistro, and Vespaio. In between, he escaped to Europe to learn more about butchery, cheesemaking, and cooking.

It was during his time at Vespaio that he met his wife, Tamara, and the two later launched their city supper club, Dai Due. (An Italian saying that translates to "from the two kingdoms of nature, choose food with care.") They later opened a butcher commissary for preparing charcuterie and prepared goods like mustards, rendered duck fat, and seasonal sausages to sell at the city's downtown farmers' market.

In 2012, Griffiths wrote *Afield,* his James Beard-nominated tome and guide to preparing wild game and fish that would become a locavore holy book. The book was a precursor to opening the Dai Due restaurant and butcher shop in 2014 with its daily menu of seasonal dishes like biscuits and venison sausage gravy, house-made pastrami and sauerkraut sandwiches, and hamberguesa (Mexican hamburgers with griddled ham and melted cheese).

Griffiths takes his cue from those who came before him, namely the Germans and Czechs who settled in the region in the late 1800s, and the Native American, Mexican, and Cajun French who were in that part of Texas long before.

"It's hard to deny the influence of those cultures in Central Texas," says Griffiths. "The Germans and the Czechs brought smoking here. That's something that's deeply rooted in our identity in Central Texas when it comes to food. It's barbecue heroes like Aaron Franklin, the Mueller family, and the pitmasters before them who solidified that flavor for us."

"We're strict about only using fresh ingredients when they're available for the particular season. If onions aren't in season, we don't use them. But we hold on to those flavors as long as possible, stored fermented, canned, dried, or pickled."

Hunting, fishing, and foraging strengthens his perpetual curiosity and commitment to seasonality. "There was a time after World War II when all of our food became industrialized and ended up in a can. We became slaves to recipes using foods that weren't even natural. That was a turning point in our history when we gave up finding what our identity was here," says Griffiths. "I want Central Texas food to have an identity. It's part of who we are."

"If onions aren't in season, we don't use them. But we hold on to those flavors as long as possible, stored fermented, canned, dried, or pickled."

TURKEY CUTLETS WITH MUSHROOM GRAVY

These breaded cutlets are a delicious way to ease into the preparation of game meats. Pounded thin, breaded, and pan-fried, these tender cuts are served with a rich sauce and are sure win over anyone. The method doesn't have to be limited to turkey breasts. It also is great for venison, feral hog loin and leg muscles, thinly sliced and pounded, or even duck or goose breasts, skinned and flattened. The mushroom gravy pairs nicely with most game.

Makes *6 servings* · **Hands-on** *30 min.* · **Total** *30 min.*

1 large egg, beaten
½ cup milk
1 cup plus 2 Tbsp. all-purpose flour, divided
1 (1½-lb.) skinned and boned turkey
    breast, cut into 6 (¼-inch-thick) slices
½ tsp. kosher salt
½ tsp. freshly ground black pepper
3 cups soft, fresh or fine, dry breadcrumbs
¼ cup unsalted butter
12 oz. assorted mushrooms, quartered
    (such as oyster and cremini)

2 garlic cloves, chopped
1 cup chicken broth
1 cup heavy cream
Pinch of ground nutmeg
1 Tbsp. fresh lemon juice
½ cup olive oil
Lemon wedges
Garnish: purslane or watercress leaves

1. Whisk together egg and milk in a shallow bowl. Place 1 cup flour in a separate shallow bowl. Sprinkle turkey with salt and pepper. Dredge turkey in flour, dip in egg mixture, and dredge in breadcrumbs, pressing gently to adhere.
2. Melt butter in a saucepan over medium-high heat; add mushrooms, and cook, stirring occasionally, 5 minutes or until lightly browned. Add garlic, and cook 30 seconds. Stir in remaining 2 Tbsp. flour.
3. Gradually stir in broth, stirring constantly to avoid lumps. Bring to a light boil; reduce heat, and add cream and nutmeg. Simmer 5 minutes or until thickened. Remove from heat, and stir in lemon juice and kosher salt and freshly ground pepper to taste. Keep warm.
4. Cook turkey, in batches, in hot oil in a large skillet over medium-high heat 3 minutes on each side or until golden brown and done. Transfer to a paper towel-lined baking sheet. Serve turkey with mushroom sauce and lemon wedges.

BEER-POACHED GRILLED SAUSAGES WITH SWEET ONIONS

It's hard to beat a great German sausage. Particularly popular in the fall at Central Texas festivals like Fredericksburg's Oktoberfest and New Braunfels' WurstFest, my preference is venison sausage, but a nice pork and beef blend is second runner-up. I like to poach the links in beer before grilling them, preferably in a local brew like Shiner Bock, like I did here, or Real Ale Fireman's No. 4 Blonde Ale. You may use your favorite brand of barbecue sauce for this recipe or a good-quality German mustard. Be sure to buy large (8- to 10-inch) tortillas so the sausages and filling will fit. For added flavor, you can also grill the tortillas.

Makes *6 servings* · **Hands-on** *20 min.* · **Total** *1 hour, including rub*

Vegetable cooking spray
6 smoked venison or pork sausage links*
4 (12-oz.) bottles lager beer
1 medium-size sweet onion, cut into
 ½-inch slices

1 tsp. Texas Meat Rub (page 13), divided
6 large flour tortillas
Barbecue sauce or coarse-grained mustard
Garnish: grilled whole chile peppers

1. Coat cold cooking grate of grill with cooking spray, Preheat grill to 350° to 400°F (medium-high) heat.
2. Bring sausages and beer to a light boil in a Dutch oven; reduce heat to medium-low, and simmer 30 to 40 minutes or until sausages are plump.
3. Meanwhile, coat both sides of onion slices with cooking spray, and sprinkle with Texas Meat Rub.
4. Grill onion slices, covered with grill lid, 8 minutes on each side or until tender and slightly charred. Transfer onion to a bowl; cover with plastic wrap, and let steam.
5. Remove sausages from beer. Grill sausages, without grill lid, 12 to 14 minutes or until thoroughly cooked, turning occasionally. (The sausages will have absorbed some of the beer while poaching, so be mindful of flare-ups.)
6. Remove sausages from grill, and let stand 3 to 4 minutes. Cut onion slices in half. Serve sausages and onions in tortillas with barbecue sauce or mustard.

*Beef sausage may be substituted.

TEXAS TOOLS

Grill

Let's face it, you're not going to get far cooking meat in Texas without a grill. More than just the occasional device used for a weekend patio party, the grill is probably the most frequently used cooking appliance at a Texas cook's disposal. In fact, if it were somehow safe to put a charcoal grill in the kitchen, thousands of people would have done it by now. (While some may cheat with a gas grill, the serious cooks swear by charcoal.)

HERBED BEER BREAD

There is nothing wrong with cornbread, buttermilk biscuits, or white fluffy icebox rolls to accompany a leisurely Sunday supper of roasted chicken, pot roast, or bowl of warm chili, but this alternative never fails to impress. A warm, buttered slice of this hearty bread pairs nicely with a juicy steak, smoked brisket, or tender ribs. Personally, I prefer locally brewed Real Ale Fireman's No. 4, but any amber or blonde ale works nicely as well.

Makes *8 to 10 servings* · **Hands-on** *10 min.* · **Total** *2 hours, 15 min.*

3 cups self-rising flour
¹/₂ cup freshly grated Parmesan cheese
1 Tbsp. sugar
1 Tbsp. finely chopped fresh oregano
1 Tbsp. finely chopped fresh basil

1 Tbsp. finely chopped fresh thyme
1 (12-oz.) can beer, at room temperature
Plain yellow cornmeal
2 Tbsp. butter, melted

1. Preheat oven to 375°F. Stir together first 6 ingredients in large bowl until well blended. Stir in beer.
2. Dust a buttered 9- x 5-inch loaf pan with cornmeal; shake out excess. Pour batter into prepared pan; let stand 5 minutes. Drizzle with melted butter.
3. Bake at 375°F for 55 minutes or until bread is golden brown and a wooden pick inserted in center comes out clean. Cool in pan on a wire rack 10 minutes; remove from pan to wire rack, and cool completely (about 1 hour).

CREAM CHEESE KOLACHES

The kolach is perhaps the most notable culinary contribution to Texas from Czech immigrants. En route to Dallas, Central Texans don't usually pass the town of West without a quick detour to the famed Czech Stop off I-35. Heading to Houston, La Grange's Weikel's Bakery and Ellinger's Hruska's are the obligatory kolach stops.

Makes *16 servings* · **Hands-on** *50 min.* · **Total** *10 hours, 10 min., including chill time*

2 (¹/₄-oz.) envelopes active dry yeast
¹/₂ cup warm water (100° to 110°F)
1 (8-oz.) container sour cream, at room temperature
¹/₂ cup sugar
¹/₂ cup butter, melted
1 tsp. table salt
3 large eggs
4 ¹/₂ cups all-purpose flour

CREAM CHEESE FILLING
1 (8-oz.) package cream cheese, softened
6 Tbsp. sugar
1 large egg yolk
1 tsp. vanilla extract
Dash of table salt

1. Combine yeast and warm water (100° to 110°F) in a 2-cup glass measuring cup; let stand 5 minutes.
2. Stir together sour cream, sugar, butter, and salt in bowl of a heavy-duty electric stand mixer. Stir in 2 eggs and yeast mixture until well blended.
3. Add 1 cup flour to bowl, and beat at low speed, using dough hook attachment. Gradually add additional flour, 1 cup at a time, and beat at medium-low speed 5 to 6 minutes or until dough begins to leave the sides of the bowl and pull together and becomes smooth and soft. Cover bowl with lightly greased plastic wrap, and chill 8 to 24 hours.
4. Turn dough out onto a well-floured surface. Shape into 16 (2-inch) balls (about ¹/₃ cup per ball), using floured hands. Place 1 ¹/₂ inches apart on 2 buttered baking sheets.
5. Cover dough with lightly greased plastic wrap, and let rise in a warm place (80° to 85°F), free from drafts, 1 hour or until doubled in bulk.
6. Prepare Cream Cheese Filling: Beat cream cheese and next 4 ingredients at medium speed with an electric mixer until smooth.
7. Preheat oven to 350°F. Press thumb or end of a wooden spoon into each dough ball, forming an indentation; fill each with 1 ¹/₂ Tbsp. Cream Cheese Filling. Whisk together 2 Tbsp. water and remaining egg in a bowl. Brush over dough.
8. Bake at 350°F for 10 minutes, placing 1 pan on middle oven rack and other on lower oven rack. Switch pans, and bake 10 to 15 more minutes or until golden.

SAUSAGE KLOBASNIKY

The sweet fruit and cream cheese version of these pastries are called "kolaches," while the savory version using sausage is referred to as a "klobasniky" or a "pig in a blanket." For added smoky flavor, grill the sausages in advance.

Makes *16 servings* · **Hands-on** *40 min.* · **Total** *11 hours, including chill time*

2 (¹/₄-oz.) envelopes active dry yeast
¹/₂ cup warm water (100° to 110°F)
1 (8-oz.) container sour cream, at room
    temperature
¹/₂ cup sugar
¹/₂ cup butter, melted

1 tsp. table salt
3 large eggs
4 ¹/₂ cups all-purpose flour
2 (12-oz.) packages smoked beef or pork
    sausage, cut into 1-inch pieces

1. Combine yeast and warm water (100° to 110°F) in a 2-cup glass measuring cup; let stand 5 minutes.
2. Stir together sour cream, sugar, butter, and salt in bowl of a heavy-duty electric stand mixer. Stir in 2 eggs and yeast mixture until well blended.
3. Add 1 cup flour to bowl, and beat at low speed, using dough hook attachment. Gradually add additional flour, 1 cup at a time, and beat at medium-low speed 5 to 6 minutes or until dough begins to leave the sides of the bowl and pull together and becomes smooth and soft. Cover bowl with lightly greased plastic wrap, and chill 8 to 24 hours.
4. Turn dough out onto a well-floured surface. Shape into 16 (2-inch) balls (about ¹/₃ cup per ball), using floured hands. Place 1 ¹/₂ inches apart on 2 buttered baking sheets.
5. Cover dough with lightly greased plastic wrap, and let rise in a warm place (80° to 85°F), free from drafts, 1 hour or until doubled in bulk.
6. Cook sausage in a large skillet over medium-high heat 6 to 8 minutes or until browned; drain on paper towels. Let cool to room temperature (about 20 minutes).
7. Press thumb or end of a wooden spoon into each dough ball, forming an indentation; fill each with 3 sausage pieces. Fold dough up and over sausage, and pinch together. Place, seam sides down, on baking sheets.
8. Whisk together 2 Tbsp. water and remaining egg. Brush over dough. Let rise 30 minutes.
9. Preheat oven to 350°F. Bake at 350°F for 10 minutes, placing 1 pan on middle oven rack and other on lower oven rack. Switch pans, and bake 10 to 15 more minutes or until golden.

GRANDMA'S COFFEE CAKE

Growing up, special family breakfasts always included this coffee cake. It originally came from the kitchen of Deer Valley Ranch in Buena Vista, Colorado, where we often escaped the Texas heat in the summertime. It's a pretty simple recipe that we've kept on file for an easy Saturday morning with family or friends. Serve with crisp bacon, scrambled eggs, and a fresh fruit salad and your morning is complete.

Makes *8 to 10 servings* · **Hands-on** *20 min.* · **Total** *2 hours, 20 min.*

2 1/2 cups all-purpose flour
3/4 cup granulated sugar
3/4 cup firmly packed light brown sugar
3/4 cup butter, melted
1 tsp. ground cinnamon
1/2 tsp. table salt

1 tsp. baking powder
3/4 tsp. baking soda
1 cup buttermilk
1 tsp. vanilla extract
1 large egg, lightly beaten
3/4 cup chopped toasted pecans, divided

1. Preheat oven to 350°F. Stir together first 6 ingredients in a bowl. (Mixture will be very crumbly.) Reserve 1/2 cup mixture. Add baking powder and baking soda to remaining flour mixture.
2. Whisk together buttermilk, vanilla, and egg in another large bowl. Stir flour mixture into buttermilk mixture just until dry ingredients are moistened. (Mixture will be slightly lumpy.) Stir in 1/2 cup pecans.
3. Pour batter into a buttered and floured 9-inch springform pan. Sprinkle with reserved flour mixture and remaining pecans.
4. Bake at 350°F for 45 to 50 minutes or until a wooden pick inserted in center comes out clean. Cool in pan on a wire rack 15 minutes; remove sides of pan, and cool completely (about 1 hour).

TEXAS TIDBIT

TEXAS STATE TREE

Georgia may be the biggest producer of pecans in the U.S., but this distinctive nut was discovered by Spanish explorers as they moved from Mexico into Texas. Many of the native Texas tribes that lived along the coast, including the Karankawa and the Coahuiltecans, feasted on Central Texas pecans along the riverbanks in the fall. In 1919, the humble pecan tree was recognized as the state tree of Texas.

LEMON-LAVENDER POUND CAKE

Hill Country growers are producing acres and acres of lavender for edible, botanical, and decorative uses, giving the heart of Texas a Provençal look. This family recipe was developed with Texas lavender fields in mind, and it's an excellent addition to a brunch or tea party.

Makes *12 to 16 servings* · **Hands-on** *20 min.* · **Total** *3 hours, 15 min.*

2 tsp. dried lavender buds
2 ³/₄ cups sugar
1 cup butter, softened
¹/₄ cup lavender honey*
6 large eggs
2 tsp. firmly packed lemon zest

1 tsp. vanilla extract
3 cups all-purpose flour
¹/₂ tsp. table salt
¹/₄ tsp. baking soda
1 cup sour cream

1. Preheat oven to 325°F. Pulse lavender and 2 Tbsp. sugar in a spice grinder until lavender is finely ground; transfer to a bowl. Stir in remaining sugar.
2. Beat butter at medium speed with a heavy-duty electric stand mixer until creamy. Gradually add lavender mixture and honey; beat at medium speed 3 to 5 minutes or until light and fluffy. Add eggs, 1 at a time, beating just until blended after each addition. Stir in lemon zest and vanilla.
3. Combine flour, salt, and baking soda. Add flour mixture to butter mixture alternately with sour cream, beginning and ending with flour mixture. Beat at low speed just until blended after each addition. Pour batter into a buttered and floured 10-inch Bundt pan.
4. Bake at 325°F for 1 hour and 15 minutes to 1 hour and 20 minutes or until a long wooden pick inserted in center comes out clean, shielding with aluminum foil after 45 to 50 minutes to prevent excessive browning. Cool in pan on a wire rack 10 minutes; remove cake from pan to wire rack, and cool completely (about 1 ¹/₂ hours).

*Regular honey may be substituted for lavender honey.

TEXAS SHEET CAKE

Somehow Texas claimed the sheet cake as its own in the mid-20th century, perhaps because of the pecans in the frosting, an ingredient that grows in abundance throughout the Lone Star State. The defining element is a large baking sheet or jelly-roll pan for baking . . . and the frosting, which has to be heated and poured on the cake while the cake is warm out of the oven. The result is a rich, chocolaty treat that's synonymous with Texas.

Makes *24 servings* · **Hands-on** *20 min.* · **Total** *2 hours, including frosting*

1 ¹/₂ cups spicy cola soft drink,
    such as Dr Pepper
1 cup vegetable or canola oil
¹/₂ cup unsweetened cocoa
2 cups all-purpose flour
1 cup granulated sugar
1 cup firmly packed light brown sugar
1 ¹/₂ tsp. baking soda
¹/₂ tsp. table salt
¹/₂ cup buttermilk
2 large eggs, lightly beaten

2 tsp. vanilla extract

FUDGE FROSTING
¹/₂ cup butter
¹/₂ (4-oz.) unsweetened chocolate baking
    bar, chopped
3 Tbsp. milk
3 Tbsp. spicy cola soft drink
4 cups powdered sugar
1 tsp. vanilla extract
1 ¹/₄ cups chopped toasted pecans

1. Preheat oven to 350°F. Bring first 3 ingredients to a boil in a medium saucepan over medium-high heat, stirring often. Remove from heat.
2. Whisk together flour and next 4 ingredients in a large bowl until blended; add warm soft drink mixture. Whisk in buttermilk, eggs, and vanilla. Pour batter into a lightly greased 17 ¹/₂- x 12 ¹/₂-inch jelly-roll pan.
3. Bake at 350°F for 18 to 22 minutes or until a wooden pick inserted in center comes out clean.
4. Prepare Fudge Frosting: Heat butter and chocolate in a medium saucepan over medium-low heat, stirring constantly until melted and smooth. Remove from heat and whisk in milk and soft drink until blended. Stir in sugar and vanilla. Beat at medium speed with an electric mixer until smooth and sugar dissolves. Pour over warm cake, spreading gently to edges. Sprinkle with chopped pecans. Cool completely in pan (about 1 hour).

TEXAS TIDBIT

DRINK OF DUBLIN

Dublin, Texas, is famous for Dr Pepper. The popular soda was introduced in Waco in 1885 and was produced by the Dublin Bottling Works in 1891. Made with pure sugar cane, this soft drink has a special place in the heart of Texans. A 2012 dispute with the parent company of the brand forced Dublin Bottling Works to remove "Dr Pepper" from its name. While the plant still makes the same particular soda, distribution is limited to a 44-mile radius of Dublin.

ORCHARD PEACH CRISP

When choosing between pies, cobblers, and crisps, I'll take crisps—thanks to their abundance of brown sugar and butter. I love their rustic texture and easy preparation too. In the summer, when Texas peaches are plentiful throughout the Hill Country, it's time to put a peach crisp together. My friend Stacey shared this recipe with me years ago, and it has never let me down.

Makes *8 to 10 servings* · **Hands-on** *15 min.* · **Total** *1 hour, 30 min.*

8 cups sliced peeled ripe peaches
$\frac{1}{2}$ cup granulated sugar
1 $\frac{1}{2}$ Tbsp. cornstarch
1 Tbsp. fresh lemon juice

1 cup firmly packed brown sugar
1 cup all-purpose flour
$\frac{1}{2}$ cup cold butter, cut into pieces
1 cup uncooked regular oats

1. Preheat oven to 375°F. Combine first 4 ingredients in a large bowl until peaches are well coated. Pour mixture into a lightly greased 13- x 9-inch baking dish.

2. Combine brown sugar and flour in a large bowl; cut in butter with a fork or pastry blender until mixture resembles coarse crumbs; stir in oats. Sprinkle over peach mixture.

3. Bake at 375°F for 1 hour and 5 minutes to 1 hour and 10 minutes or until topping is golden brown and center is bubbly. Cool 10 minutes before serving.

TEXAS TIDBIT

HILL COUNTRY PEACHES

Among the many natural resources of the Texas Hill Country, the limestone-laced soils near Fredericksburg proved the perfect mix for peaches. In the 1800s, German immigrants cultivated numerous peach orchards in the area. By the early 1900s, it was reported that there were more than 10 million peach trees in Texas, with many family orchards bearing the German heritage in their name including Vogel, Engel, Inman, Berg, and Studebaker.

CHAPTER TWO

EAST
★ TEXAS ★

Texas' roots as part of the Deep South begin in East Texas. While French exploration occurred in the late 1600s, settlement didn't really take place until the 1800s, and while the food in the area shows influences of the French-Cajun areas of nearby Louisiana, signature Southern flavors predominate. The borders of East Texas extend south through Beaumont and west toward Dallas, stopping short of Fort Worth. Much of the food reflects this Southern culture with a variety of traditional dishes gracing the table.

PIMIENTO CHEESE

Light on the mayonnaise, heavy on sharp Cheddar and roasted red peppers, this version of the quintessential Southern dip is so addictive it's good on just about anything.

Makes *2 cups* · **Hands-on** *15 min.* · **Total** *15 min.*

4 oz. cream cheese, softened
$^1/_4$ cup mayonnaise
1 tsp. Worcestershire sauce
$^1/_2$ tsp. sherry vinegar
1 cup (4 oz.) shredded pepper Jack cheese
1 cup (4 oz.) shredded extra-sharp
    Cheddar cheese

1 Tbsp. grated onion
$^1/_4$ tsp. kosher salt
Freshly ground black pepper to taste
$^1/_2$ (12-oz.) jar roasted red peppers, drained
    and finely chopped*

Beat first 4 ingredients at medium speed with an electric mixer until smooth. Stir in remaining ingredients. Cover and chill until ready to serve. Refrigerate in an airtight container up to 1 week.

Note: To roast fresh red bell peppers, arrange on an aluminum foil-lined baking sheet and broil 5 inches from heat 5 to 10 minutes on each side or until bell peppers look charred and blistered. Transfer bell peppers to a heavy-duty zip-top plastic bag; seal and let stand 10 minutes to loosen skins. Peel, remove and discard seeds, and finely chop.

TEXAS TIDBIT

CLASSIC TEXAS SAYINGS

*Timid: He wouldn't
bite a biscuit.
Dry: It's so dry the catfish
are carrying canteens.
Loud: Noisy as a restless
mule in a tin barn.
Hot: So hot the hens are
laying hard-boiled eggs.
Sad: He looks like the cheese
fell off his cracker.*

BROWN SUGAR BACON

When you're staring down at a plate of hot, crispy bacon on a Saturday morning, it's hard to imagine anything better, but something pretty spectacular happens when you mix some sweet in with the salty. For this recipe, the last few minutes are critical. Watch the bacon closely to make sure it doesn't burn.

Makes *12 to 18 bacon slices* · **Hands-on** *10 min.* · **Total** *35 min.*

1 ¹/₂ cups firmly packed light brown sugar   1 (12-oz.) package center-cut bacon

1. Preheat oven to 350°F. Line 2 (16- x 11-inch) jelly-roll pans with aluminum foil; place lightly greased wire racks on top of foil.
2. Spread brown sugar in an even layer in a shallow dish. Dredge bacon in sugar, turning each slice 3 or 4 times, and pressing lightly to coat bacon generously with sugar. Arrange bacon slices in a single layer on wire racks, leaving about a ¹/₂-inch space between slices.
3. Bake at 350°F for 20 to 30 minutes or until lightly browned. Cool on racks in pans 5 minutes or until crisp.

SOUTHWEST CORNMEAL BACON

Makes *12 bacon slices* · **Hands-on** *10 min.* · **Total** *55 min.*

Preheat oven to 350°F. Stir together ¹/₃ cup plain yellow cornmeal, ¹/₄ cup firmly packed light brown sugar, ¹/₄ tsp. ground cumin, and ¹/₄ tsp. ground red pepper. Dredge 12 thick bacon slices in cornmeal mixture, shaking off excess. Arrange bacon in a single layer on a wire rack coated with vegetable cooking spray; place in an aluminum foil-lined jelly-roll pan. Bake at 350°F for 40 to 50 minutes or until crisp.

BBQ BACON

Makes *12 bacon slices* · **Hands-on** *10 min.* · **Total** *55 min.*

Preheat oven to 350°F. Stir together 5 Tbsp. light brown sugar, 1 Tbsp. chili powder, 1 tsp. ground cumin, and ¹/₄ tsp. ground red pepper. Dredge 12 thick bacon slices in sugar mixture, pressing to adhere. Arrange bacon in a single layer on a wire rack coated with vegetable cooking spray; place in an aluminum foil-lined jelly-roll pan. Bake at 350°F for 40 to 50 minutes or until crisp.

BLACK-EYED PEAS

Southerners have long considered this little one-eyed legume a side-dish staple, especially to ring in the New Year with a serving of luck. Simmered a few hours with salt pork, onions, and a little tomato paste, this is a delicious side dish to serve throughout the whole year. The Lone Star spin adds an assertive Texas kick.

Makes *8 cups* · **Hands-on** *15 min.* · **Total** *10 hours, 15 min.*

1 (16-oz.) package dried black-eyed peas
1 ½ cups chopped onion
¼ cup tomato paste
½ lb. smoked ham hocks
1 Tbsp. minced fresh garlic

1 tsp. freshly ground black pepper
1 jalapeño pepper, chopped
2 tsp. table salt, divided
1 Tbsp. Worcestershire sauce
Hot sauce

1. Rinse and sort peas according to package directions. Place peas in a Dutch oven; cover with cold water 2 inches above peas, and let soak 8 hours. Drain peas, and rinse thoroughly.
2. Bring peas, onion, next 5 ingredients, 1 tsp. salt, and 1 qt. water to a boil in Dutch oven over medium-high heat; cover, reduce heat to low, and simmer, stirring occasionally, 1 hour. Uncover and stir in remaining 1 tsp. salt. Simmer, uncovered, 30 minutes to 1 hour or until peas are tender.
3. Stir in Worcestershire sauce, and add salt and pepper to taste. Serve with hot sauce.

Note: We tested with Tabasco sauce.

TEXAS TIDBIT

THE LUCK OF THE BLACK-EYED PEA

While many historians have traced the origins of the humble pea's good fortune to ancient Egyptians and Babylonian times, Athens' historical record reveals that the late Elmore Rural Torn of Taylor, Texas, founder of the International Black-Eyed Pea Appreciation Society and father of actor Rip Torn, said that certain Asiatic, African, and European cultures ate black-eyed peas to protect them from the Evil Eye. Though the little legume has widely been consumed throughout the South for quite some time, it's Torn who is credited with the revival of the good-luck meal across the country when served on New Year's Day.

FRESH OKRA AND TOMATOES

There are many renditions of stewed okra and tomatoes: from long simmered with bacon and onions to stewed in a flavorful roux with andouille sausage, shrimp, or crab, Creole-style. While these long-simmered versions have their place, I prefer the freshness of the tomatoes and okra in this simple, quick-cooking recipe—especially when okra is in season. Serve it mild if you'd like, or turn up the heat with a shot or two of hot sauce.

Makes *4 to 6 servings* · **Hands-on** *35 min.* · **Total** *35 min.*

1 small onion, chopped
2 Tbsp. olive oil
2 garlic cloves, minced
1 lb. fresh okra, sliced

½ tsp. table salt
5 large plum tomatoes, diced
2 tsp. Creole seasoning
Hot sauce (optional)

Sauté onion in hot oil in a large skillet over medium heat 5 to 6 minutes or until tender and beginning to brown. Add garlic, and sauté 1 minute. Add okra and salt, and cook 3 minutes or until okra begins to soften. Stir in tomatoes and Creole seasoning, and cook 5 minutes or until okra is tender. Add salt and freshly ground black pepper to taste and, if desired, hot sauce.

Note: We tested with Tony Cachere's Creole Seasoning.

KENTUCKY WONDER BEANS

It's true, my favorite green bean varietal gets cooked for an unbelievable amount of time here, but the addition of cooked, crisp bacon balances the beans' silky texture and a whole lot of black pepper makes them extraordinary. If you can't find this bean variety, substitute your favorite.

Makes *6 to 8 servings* · **Hands-on** *30 min.* · **Total** *2 hours, 30 min.*

8 bacon slices
1 medium onion, thinly sliced
4 garlic cloves, minced
1 bay leaf
2 fresh thyme sprigs
2 lb. fresh green beans (such as Kentucky Wonders), trimmed

1 tsp. table salt
1 tsp. freshly ground black pepper
1/4 tsp. dried crushed red pepper (optional)
1 cup chicken broth
2 Tbsp. apple cider vinegar

1. Cook bacon in a large Dutch oven over medium-low heat 8 minutes or until crisp; remove bacon, and drain on paper towels, reserving 2 Tbsp. drippings in Dutch oven and 1 Tbsp. drippings in a small bowl. Crumble bacon.
2. Increase heat to medium-high. Sauté onion, garlic, bay leaf, and thyme in hot drippings in Dutch oven 5 minutes or until onion is tender.
3. Stir in beans, salt, black pepper, and, if desired, crushed red pepper. Add broth and reserved 1 Tbsp. bacon drippings, and bring to a boil. Cover, reduce heat, and simmer, stirring occasionally, 2 hours to 2 hours and 15 minutes or until beans are tender.
4. Remove from heat, and discard thyme and bay leaf. Stir in vinegar and crumbled bacon. Serve warm or at room temperature.

BOURBON SWEET POTATOES

Turkey with stuffing is just fine for Thanksgiving, but nothing comes close to a serving of these bourbon-spiked sweet spuds. As a kid, my uncle once told me I couldn't have any because they had "firewater" in them. I'm pretty sure that was so he could have more for himself. Some people like a sticky marshmallow topping, but I think this version is a much better way to add a little spunk to the humble yam.

Makes *6 to 8 servings* · **Hands-on** *20 min.* · **Total** *2 hours, 45 min.*

3 large sweet potatoes
$1/2$ cup sugar
$1/4$ cup butter, melted
$1/4$ cup bourbon, such as Garrison Brothers
    Texas Straight Bourbon Whiskey

$1/4$ tsp. ground cinnamon
$1/4$ tsp. ground nutmeg
$1/8$ tsp. ground cloves
2 large eggs
1 (5-oz.) can evaporated milk

1. Preheat oven to 375°F. Place potatoes on a baking sheet; bake at 375°F for 1 hour or until tender. Cool slightly (about 15 minutes).
2. Reduce oven temperature to 350°F. Peel potatoes, and mash with a potato masher until smooth. Stir in sugar and remaining ingredients until well blended and smooth. Spoon mixture into lightly greased 11- x 7-inch baking dish.
3. Bake at 350°F for 1 hour and 10 minutes or until a wooden pick inserted in center comes out clean.

PIMIENTO CHEESE GRITS

This recipe brings together two Southern classics: creamy pimiento cheese and rustic country grits. It's a perfect side dish for grilled meats or Shrimp Creole (page 127).

Makes *4 cups* · **Hands-on** *10 min.* · **Total** *35 min.*

4 cups reduced-sodium fat-free
   chicken broth
1 cup uncooked regular grits

1 Tbsp. minced fresh garlic
1 cup Pimiento Cheese (page 54)
¼ cup butter

1. Bring chicken broth to a boil in a medium saucepan over medium-high heat. Gradually add grits, whisking constantly. Whisk in garlic.
2. Bring to a boil; reduce heat to medium-low, and simmer, whisking occasionally, 20 minutes or until tender and thickened. Remove from heat.
3. Add Pimiento Cheese and butter, whisking until cheese is melted and mixture is well blended. Add salt and freshly ground black pepper to taste. Serve immediately.

CREAMY GARLIC MASHED POTATOES

What Sunday roast or thick-cut pork chop is complete without a healthy heap of mashed potatoes? I've had all sorts of renditions— from rosemary to blue cheese to Parmesan and even Ranch-flavored mashed potatoes—but you really can't get much better than mashed potatoes made with loads of sweet butter and garlic. Be sure to leave the skins on when you boil the potatoes because they prevent the potatoes from absorbing too much water.

Makes *6 to 8 servings* · **Hands-on** *20 min.* · **Total** *40 min.*

2 lb. red potatoes, quartered
1 Tbsp. table salt
1 cup heavy cream
¼ cup chicken broth

6 Tbsp. butter
1 Tbsp. minced garlic
½ cup sour cream

1. Bring potatoes, salt, and water to cover to a boil in a large saucepan over medium heat, and cook 15 to 20 minutes or until tender. Drain. Return potatoes to pan. Cook over medium heat, stirring occasionally, 1 minute or until potatoes are dry; mash with a potato masher to desired consistency.
2. Meanwhile, bring cream, broth, butter, and garlic to a light boil over medium heat in a saucepan, stirring occasionally. (Do not boil.)
3. Gently stir one-third of hot cream mixture into potatoes, stirring just until blended. Gradually stir in half of remaining cream mixture, adding additional hot cream mixture for desired consistency. Str in sour cream. Add salt and freshly ground black pepper to taste.

GRANDMA'S MEATLOAF

Meatloaf wasn't exactly a welcomed dish in my household growing up. Neither of my folks had sampled a meatloaf that wasn't dry, tasteless, or slathered in a blanket of ketchup. Many years later, I made an effort to give such a beloved American dish another look. This rendition is what made me love meatloaf. In truth, it is not my grandma's meatloaf, but I cherish it as if it were.

Makes *6 servings* · **Hands-on** *25 min.* · **Total** *1 hour, 25 min.*

3 to 4 (1-oz.) white bread slices
¹/₂ cup milk
1 small onion, chopped
1 tsp. vegetable oil
¹/₂ cup tomato paste, divided
1 large egg

2 ¹/₂ Tbsp. Worcestershire sauce, divided
1 ¹/₂ tsp. table salt, divided
¹/₄ tsp. freshly ground black pepper
1 ¹/₂ lb. ground chuck
2 Tbsp. dark brown sugar
3 Tbsp. apple cider vinegar

1. Preheat oven to 350°F. Cut crusts from bread slices; crumble bread into small pieces in a bowl. Pour milk over bread; let stand at least 5 minutes. Squeeze bread to remove excess liquid. Place bread in a large bowl.

2. Cook onion in hot oil in a skillet over medium heat 7 minutes or until tender. Add onion, ¹/₄ cup tomato paste, egg, 1 Tbsp. Worcestershire sauce, 1 tsp. salt, and pepper to bread, whisking to break up large pieces of bread.

3. Combine ground chuck and bread mixture, using hands. Shape mixture into an 8- x 2-inch loaf on an aluminum foil-lined jelly-roll pan.

4. Stir together brown sugar, vinegar, and remaining ¹/₄ cup tomato paste, 1 ¹/₂ Tbsp. Worcestershire sauce, and ¹/₂ tsp. salt; pour half of mixture over meatloaf.

5. Bake at 350°F for 30 minutes. Pour remaining half of tomato mixture over meatloaf. Bake 15 to 30 more minutes or until a meat thermometer inserted into thickest portion registers 160°F. Remove from oven; let stand 10 to 20 minutes.

TIM BYRES

CHEF/OWNER SMOKE, CHICKEN SCRATCH, THE FOUNDRY,
BAR BELMONT, DALLAS

Tim Byres was working under chef Stephan Pyles at his eponymous restaurant in Dallas when the path to his future began to take shape.

"He had a light in his eyes, and I could tell he was always trying to find ways to do things with his own intent," says Pyles. "It was really cool to watch."

With California roots and experience as a chef in Brussels, Haiti, the Mississippi Delta, and the Pacific Northwest, it was Byres mentorship by Pyles that established his connection to Texas food.

On a trip with Pyles to the west Texas town of Buffalo Gap, Byres met Tom Perini, a larger-than-life character focused on authentic cowboy cooking over big pits and roasting fires at Perini Ranch Steakhouse. Pyles and Byres were there for the annual Buffalo Gap Food and Wine Summit hosted by Perini and his wife, Lisa. The experience made a lasting impression.

"Going out to see Perini at Buffalo Gap is like going to see a lion in its native home in Africa," says Byres. "We were cooking over big campfires under the stars, and there was dancing under the shade of a live oak grove with lights strung up on the tree branches. It was the real thing. It was a place with a real sense of purpose.

"Texas is a crossroads for so many different food cultures, and it has created an identity that has drawn from all of them," says Byres. "It was a hard place to settle long ago.

Everything about it was difficult. It was the Wild West. As a result, Texas food at its core is gritty. It's loud, unapologetic, high in flavor and heart, and it's all served up on a plate big enough for ranch hands to devour after a hard day of working to get back up for more."

In 2009, Byres went out on his own to open SMOKE, an upscale barbecue and Southern fare restaurant using smoke from wood-fired pits and ovens as the key element for cooking. To do it, he had to go back to the basics of Texas cooking.

"Pyles does a great job of taking his interpretation of Texas cuisine and putting it on a porcelain plate in a nice restaurant. Perini grabs a slab of steak off an open fire and serves it up on a tin plate next to a spoonful of beans. I wanted to do something in between," says Byres. "SMOKE is about taking a new approach to fire cooking. We take the same flavors you'd find in the Deep South or in Mexican food and apply that to meats and side dishes. The common thread is always the smoke. It's about taking food back all the way to when they just had a fire on the ground. That's where the true grit of Texas food comes from."

Byres may not be a Texas native, but his dedication and earnest approach in uncovering the true grit of Texas cooking has made him a Texan for the rest of his life. "I've always believed you've got to bloom where you're planted," says Byres. "I'm just glad I was able to plant myself here."

"We were cooking over big campfires under the stars, and there was dancing under the shade of a live oak grove ... It was the real thing. It was a place with a real sense of purpose."

TIM BYRES' PORK CHOPS WITH APRICOT-MUSTARD SAUCE

Chef Tim Byres of Dallas' SMOKE restaurant makes his pork chops by slow cooking an entire rib roast over indirect heat first before cutting it into individual chops and finishing them over direct heat on the grill. The result is something pretty magical. This is his recipe for pork chops from his 2013 James Beard Award-winning cookbook, SMOKE: New Firewood Cooking *as well as the sides he typically serves with them.*

Makes *8 to 10 servings ·* **Hands-on** *10 min. ·* **Total** *3 hours, 50 min., including sauce*

¹/₃ to ¹/₂ cup Texas Meat Rub (page 13)
1 (7 ¹/₂- to 8-lb.) bone-in pork loin roast

APRICOT-MUSTARD SAUCE
1 ¹/₂ cups dried apricots
2 Tbsp. sherry vinegar
2 Tbsp. red wine vinegar
2 Tbsp. Dijon mustard
1 tsp. kosher salt

1. Rub Texas Meat Rub over roast. Let stand at room temperature 1 hour.
2. Light 1 side of grill, heating to 325° to 350°F (medium) heat; leave other side unlit. Place pork, bone side down, over unlit side, and grill, covered with grill lid, 2 to 2 ¹/₂ hours or until a meat thermometer inserted into thickest portion registers 145°F.
3. Prepare Apricot-Mustard Sauce: Bring apricots and 3 cups water to a light boil over medium heat; reduce heat, and simmer 15 to 20 minutes or until apricots are plump and soft. Stir in remaining ingredients, and cook 2 minutes. Remove from heat.
4. Process mixture with an immersion blender until smooth. (A regular blender may be used. Let sauce cool slightly before blending.) Season with salt to taste.
5. Remove roast from grill and let stand 20 minutes before cutting into individual chops. Serve with Apricot-Mustard Sauce.

RUMP ROAST

The holidays at my grandmother's home always had a few country menu standards like green beans, mashed potatoes, fruit salad, and classic rump roast. I have always savored the simplicity of this juicy Texas beef roast with its tasty pan drippings. I assumed it would be difficult to duplicate on my own, but with the Texas Meat Rub (page 13) on hand, I can make this roast without referencing a recipe. Leftovers are great on sandwiches or in tacos.

Makes *8 to 10 servings* · **Hands-on** *10 min.* · **Total** *2 hours, 40 min., including rub*

1 (3- to 4-lb.) boneless beef rump roast, trimmed
1 ½ Tbsp. olive oil, divided

3 Tbsp. Texas Meat Rub (page 13)
1 large yellow or sweet onion, thinly sliced
¼ cup Worcestershire sauce

1. Cut 10 slits in roast at 1-inch intervals, using a sharp knife. Rub roast with 1 Tbsp. oil and Texas Meat Rub, pushing rub into slits. Place roast in a large cast-iron skillet or roasting pan. Let roast come to room temperature (about 1 to 2 hours).
2. Preheat oven to 375°F. Combine onion and remaining 1 ½ tsp. oil. Top roast with onion and Worcestershire sauce.
3. Bake at 375°F for 1 hour and 15 minutes or until beef is tender. Let roast stand 10 to 15 minutes. Cut roast against the grain into thin slices with a sharp knife. Serve immediately with onions.

MONUMENT CAFE CHICKEN-FRIED STEAK

Chicken-fried steak originated in Texas. It was most likely created around where East and Central Texas meet. This is the place where traditional Southern deep-fried foods melded with the batter-dipped German-style schnitzel. Many roadside stops throughout the state claim to have the best chicken-fried steak. One of my favorites is found just north of Austin in Georgetown at the Monument Cafe, where owner Rusty Winkstern has made this Texas classic an art form.

Makes *4 servings* · **Hands-on** *50 min.* · **Total** *1 hour, 50 min.*

2 tsp. kosher salt, divided
1 tsp. freshly ground black pepper, divided
³/₄ tsp. ground red pepper, divided
4 (4-oz.) cubed steaks
2 large eggs
1 cup buttermilk

2 cups all-purpose flour, divided
2 tsp. seasoned salt, such as Lawry's, divided
¹/₂ cup canola oil
2 cups milk

1. Combine 1 tsp. kosher salt, ¹/₂ tsp. black pepper, and ¹/₄ tsp. red pepper in a bowl. Sprinkle cubed steaks with mixture, and place on a paper towel-lined baking sheet. Whisk eggs and buttermilk in a shallow dish. Let steaks and buttermilk mixture come to room temperature (about 1 hour).
2. Meanwhile, combine 1 cup flour, 1 tsp. seasoned salt, ¹/₂ tsp. kosher salt, ¹/₄ tsp. black pepper, and ¹/₄ tsp. red pepper in a shallow dish; repeat with remaining flour, seasoned salt, kosher salt, black pepper, and red pepper in a second shallow dish. Reserve 3 Tbsp. flour mixture from 1 bowl.
3. Dredge steaks in flour mixture, dip in egg mixture, and dredge in flour mixture; shake off excess.
4. Heat oil in a 12-inch skillet over medium-high to 325°F. Fry steaks, in batches, 2 to 3 minutes on each side or until golden. Drain on a wire rack in a jelly-roll pan. Reserve 3 Tbsp. drippings in skillet.
5. Whisk 3 Tbsp. reserved flour mixture into hot drippings in skillet until smooth. Cook over medium-high heat, whisking constantly, 30 seconds or until bubbly and light brown. Gradually whisk in milk; cook, whisking constantly, 5 minutes or until mixture is thickened. Sprinkle with kosher salt and freshly ground black pepper to taste, if desired. Serve steaks with gravy.

Note: We tested with Lawry's Seasoned Salt.

CHICKEN AND DUMPLINGS

Perhaps one of the greatest of Southern comfort foods, chicken and dumplings is something I crave when the weather turns cold. My mom's chicken and dumplings are hard to beat, though her recipe comes from the side of the biscuit mix box. So often dumplings can be gummy and dense, but I've found the addition of cornmeal adds a nice texture.

Makes *6 to 8 servings* · **Hands-on** *45 min.* · **Total** *1 hour, 40 min.*

4 (8-oz.) skin-on, bone-in chicken breasts, skinned
2 ¹/₂ tsp. table salt, divided
1 tsp. freshly ground black pepper
6 cups chicken broth
¹/₄ cup butter
1 cup diced carrots
1 cup diced celery
1 cup diced onion
1 tsp. dried thyme
2 ¹/₂ cups milk, divided
1 ³/₄ cups all-purpose flour
³/₄ cup plain yellow or white cornmeal
2 Tbsp. finely chopped fresh parsley
1 ¹/₂ Tbsp. baking powder
Garnish: fresh thyme

1. Bring chicken, 1 tsp. salt, pepper, and broth to a boil in a large saucepan over medium heat. Cover, reduce heat to medium-low, and simmer 15 minutes or until done; remove chicken and reserve broth.
2. Cool chicken 30 minutes; skin, bone, and shred or chop chicken, discarding skin and bones. Add chicken to broth.
3. Melt butter in a stockpot over medium-high heat. Add carrots, celery, and onion; sauté 5 to 7 minutes or until vegetables are softened and lightly browned.
4. Add thyme, broth mixture, and 1 cup milk. Bring to a light boil; reduce heat, and simmer 10 to 15 minutes.
5. Meanwhile, combine flour, next 3 ingredients, and remaining 1 ¹/₂ tsp. salt and 1 ¹/₂ cups milk in a medium bowl until blended.
6. Drop dumplings, by ¹/₄ cupfuls, into simmering broth, stirring gently. (Pot will be very full.) Cover and simmer, stirring often, 15 minutes or until dumplings are done, and serve immediately.

TEXAS TOOLS

Stockpot

Let the Dutch oven and cast-iron skillet do the heavy cooking. When it comes to making soup or a homemade stock, a good, sturdy stockpot is a necessity. Depending on how many people you normally entertain, the size of your stockpot may vary. In general, a 12-qt. pot will get you started, but for serious cooking, a 20-qt. pot will never let you down.

CORNMEAL FRIED FISH

There are a number of ways to make country-style fried fish, but I like this cornmeal batter best. Be sure to keep an eye on the temperature of the oil—too low and the fish will be greasy . . . too hot and it burns quickly. Serve the fish with your favorite tartar or cocktail sauce and a pile of Homestyle Hush Puppies (page 80).

Makes *8 servings* · **Hands-on** *30 min.* · **Total** *30 min.*

$^2/_3$ cup plain yellow cornmeal
$^1/_3$ cup all-purpose flour
1 tsp. table salt
$^1/_2$ tsp. freshly ground black pepper
$^1/_4$ tsp. ground red pepper
1 large egg

$^1/_4$ cup milk
2 lb. mild white fish fillets (catfish or tilapia)
Vegetable oil
Tartar sauce
Cocktail sauce

1. Combine first 5 ingredients in a large shallow bowl. Whisk together egg and milk in a second shallow bowl.
2. Dip fish in egg mixture; dredge in cornmeal mixture, shaking off excess.
3. Pour oil to depth of 1 $^1/_2$ inches in a deep cast-iron skillet; heat to 350°F. Fry fish, in batches, 5 minutes or until golden. Drain on paper towels. Serve immediately with tartar sauce and cocktail sauce.

TEXAS PIT STOPS

FLORIDA'S KITCHEN
Livingston

STILLWATER INN
Jefferson

STANLEY'S FAMOUS PIT BBQ
Tyler

THE ZODIAC AT NEIMAN MARCUS
Dallas

CAMPISI'S EGYPTIAN RESTAURANT
Dallas

EL FENIX
Dallas

HOMESTYLE HUSH PUPPIES

I love the crisp outer coating and the inner doughiness of the cornmeal in these tasty little fritters. I like to add a little seasoning and chopped green onions to the standard cornmeal batter. These only take a few seconds, so be careful not to walk away or you may ruin a perfectly good bite.

Makes *6 to 8 servings* · **Hands-on** *20 min.* · **Total** *30 min.*

Vegetable oil
³/₄ cup plain yellow cornmeal
¹/₂ cup all-purpose flour
1 Tbsp. baking powder
1 Tbsp. sugar
1 tsp. baking soda
1 tsp. table salt

¹/₂ tsp. garlic powder
¹/₄ tsp. paprika
¹/₄ tsp. ground red pepper
³/₄ cup buttermilk
1 large egg, lightly beaten
¹/₄ cup chopped green onions
Tartar sauce

1. Pour oil to depth of 2 inches into a Dutch oven; heat to 350°F. Combine cornmeal and next 8 ingredients in a large bowl. Add buttermilk, egg, and green onions; stir just until moistened. Let stand 10 minutes (batter will be fluffy).
2. Drop batter by rounded tablespoonfuls into hot oil, and fry, in batches, 2 to 3 minutes on each side or until golden. Drain on a wire rack over paper towels. Serve immediately with tartar sauce.

STEPHAN PYLES

CHEF/RESTAURATEUR, STEPHAN PYLES, STAMPEDE 66, SAN SALVAJE, DALLAS

As a James Beard Award-winning chef, author, and TV personality, Stephan Pyles has made an indelible mark on Texas cuisine. Of the founders of Southwestern cuisine, a culinary phenomenon who swept Texas and other states throughout the Southwest in the late '80s with fellow chefs Dean Fearing, Robert Del Grande, Avner Samuel, and Amy Ferguson, he is the only Texas native.

Born in the West Texas town of Big Spring, Pyles' first experience in the kitchen was in his family's truck stop diner—something that later led him to culinary school where he fell in love with classic French cuisine.

At his first restaurant, Routh Street Cafe, his consistent success in translating the flavors of other cultures into Texas dishes drew many accolades. Pyles has gone on to open more than a dozen restaurants in the Dallas area. His namesake Stephan Pyles restaurant operates in tandem with nearby San Salvaje and Stampede 66.

Though Southwestern cooking made its debut more than three decades ago, its influences still proliferate on top Texas menus today, but as Pyles notes, there is much more emphasis on the flavors of specific regions within the state.

"When you talk about French, Indian, Mexican, or any other culture, the foods are very specific to regions. Texas is starting to see a focus on region as well, which is exciting to see," says Pyles. "It will take us further into appreciating the history of how our state came to be and the heritage that brought it to where we are today."

Getting Pyles to define Dallas cuisine, the city where he's made his career, is a bit harder to do.

"Dallas has always been a little bit of an odd duck in Texas because it was sort of invented as a mistake," says Pyles, referring to Dallas' location being far from any navigable link to the sea or other major cities. "It was really only developed because of the railroads, but that's also what makes it great. It doesn't have to be any one thing. When I came here in the '70s, there was Tex-Mex and Southern food, but the Southern styles seemed different to me than in East Texas. Everything was more fine-tuned here. The fine-tuning effect that Dallas has is what allowed things like Southwestern cuisine to make such an impact on the state."

In recent years, however, Pyles has seen a dynamic shift from modern chefs. From the local foraging of herbs and mushrooms by FT33's Matt McAllister to the fusion of Southern cuisine with grilling and smoking by Tim Byres, chefs cook food expressed through the personality and culture of what Dallas really is.

With more than 30 years under his belt as a definitive Texas chef, Pyles shows no sign of stopping. With his most recent concept, Stampede, he's joined chefs like McAllister and Byres in presenting what he is calling Modern Texas Cuisine. "All we're doing is expanding on what has been all around us for centuries. We're drawing on our own identity as a city, and that's really exciting to see. It keeps us all relevant as chefs, and allows us to celebrate the true flavors of Texas."

Stephan Pyles' Biscuits

1 1/2 Tbsp. unsalted butter
5 Tbsp. cold shortening, cut into cubes
1 1/2 cups self-rising flour
3/4 cup buttermilk

1. Preheat oven to 400°F. Melt butter in a 10-inch cast-iron skillet.
2. Cut shortening into flour with a pastry blender or fork so it resembles small peas. Add buttermilk, stirring just until dry ingredients are moistened.
3. Turn dough out onto a floured surface; knead 3 or 4 times. Pat or roll dough 3/4 inch thick; cut with a 2 1/2-inch round cutter. Place in skillet, dipping both sides of biscuits in melted butter. Repeat with scraps to make 2 more biscuits; discard remaining dough.
4. Bake at 400°F for 10 to 12 minutes or until biscuit bottoms are golden. Increase oven temperature to broil; broil 4 inches from heat 1 minute or until tops are brown. Serve immediately or transfer biscuits to a wire rack.

Makes *6 to 8 biscuits*
Hands-on *20 min.*
Total *30 min.*

HONEY-FRIED CHICKEN WITH WHITE WINE CREAM SAUCE

Chef Stephan Pyles' grandmother's secret to perfect fried chicken: Marinate pieces in honey and vinegar before frying them really slowly. Otherwise the honey will burn. Over the years, Pyles worked diligently to replicate the beloved recipe so that it takes less time. His hard work paid off. It's likely his grandmother would be proud too. It's important to cook the chicken at a low temperature to prevent the honey from caramelizing too quickly and burning.

Makes *8 to 10 servings* · **Hands-on** *1 hour, 20 min.* · **Total** *5 hours, 20 min.*

³/₄ cup honey
1¹/₂ Tbsp. apple cider vinegar or
    Champagne vinegar
1¹/₂ Tbsp. fresh orange juice
1¹/₂ tsp. fresh lemon juice
2 (3-lb.) cut-up whole chickens
³/₄ cup all-purpose flour

2 large eggs
¹/₄ cup buttermilk
Vegetable or corn oil
¹/₂ cup dry white wine
¹/₂ cup chicken broth
1 cup heavy cream

1. Combine first 4 ingredients in a large glass or ceramic bowl; add chicken. Cover and chill 4 to 8 hours, turning occasionally.
2. Remove chicken from marinade; drain on paper towels. Pour marinade through a wire-mesh strainer into a bowl, reserving 2 Tbsp. marinade. Discard remaining marinade.
3. Place flour in a shallow dish. Whisk eggs with buttermilk in a separate shallow dish. Dip chicken in egg mixture; dredge in flour, shaking off excess.
4. Pour oil to depth of 1 inch into a large cast-iron skillet; heat to 275°F. Fry chicken, in batches, turning occasionally, 15 to 20 minutes or until evenly browned and done. Drain on a wire rack over paper towels. Sprinkle with salt and freshly ground black pepper to taste while hot.
5. Remove and discard oil from skillet, reserving drippings in skillet. Add wine, and cook 2 minutes, stirring to loosen browned bits from bottom of skillet. Add broth, and simmer 8 minutes or until liquid is reduced by half. Add cream and reserved 2 Tbsp. marinade. Bring to a boil; reduce heat to medium-low, and simmer 6 minutes or until mixture thickens and coats a spoon.
6. Pour sauce through a wire-mesh strainer into a serving bowl. Add salt and freshly ground black pepper to taste. Serve with fried chicken.

SKILLET CORNBREAD

While some prefer a more savory version, I like my cornbread to have a little sweetness. The addition of honey, creamed corn, and corn kernels does just the trick. Cast-iron cooking creates crispy edges, but you can also bake this bread in muffin tins or a cake pan.

Makes *10 to 12 servings* · **Hands-on** *10 min.* · **Total** *35 min.*

1 ¼ cups finely ground stone-ground yellow cornmeal
¾ cup all-purpose flour
1 tsp. baking soda
1 tsp. baking powder
1 tsp. table salt

¾ cup frozen whole kernel corn, thawed
1 ¼ cups buttermilk
⅓ cup vegetable or canola oil
2 Tbsp. honey
2 large eggs

1. Preheat oven to 400°F. Heat a 10-inch cast-iron skillet in oven 5 minutes.
2. Stir together cornmeal and next 4 ingredients in a large bowl; stir in corn. Whisk together buttermilk and next 3 ingredients; add to cornmeal mixture, stirring just until dry ingredients are moistened. Pour batter into hot greased skillet.
3. Bake at 400°F for 25 to 30 minutes or until golden brown and a wooden pick inserted in center comes out clean.

CORNBREAD CROUTONS

Makes *4 cups* · **Hands-on** *8 min.* · **Total** *25 min.*

¼ cup butter
3 small garlic cloves, sliced
4 cups cubed Skillet Cornbread (about 1-inch cubes; recipe above)

½ tsp. dried parsley flakes
¼ tsp. table salt

1. Preheat oven to 450°F. Melt butter in a small skillet over medium heat. Add garlic; cook, stirring often, 1 to 2 minutes or until fragrant. Remove from heat; let stand 2 minutes. Remove and discard garlic.
2. Combine cornbread, parsley, salt, and garlic butter on a lightly greased jelly-roll pan, tossing gently to coat.
3. Bake at 450°F in a single layer for 15 minutes or until edges are golden, stirring every 5 minutes. Serve warm or at room temperature.

TEXAS TOOLS

Cast-Iron Skillet

You may be able to get away with frying chicken in a deep fryer, cooking a Sunday roast in a slow cooker, or serving cornbread out of a simple baking tin. But the truth is, without a good, well-seasoned cast-iron skillet (or two) in your kitchen, these dishes just don't have the soul. In Texas, it shows a lack of respect for the food.

The best way to clean one? Personally, I wipe my skillet down with a towel. Then I add a handful of kosher salt to the base and scrub it with a rag. I wipe it clean with another towel, rub a couple of tablespoons of olive oil all over it, and set it on the stove-top to dry over low heat.

CLASSIC ICEBOX ROLLS

Icebox dinner rolls are a suppertime standard across the South. My mother-in-law makes these for Sunday dinners and holiday feasts. It's also the basic dough for her Icebox Cinnamon Rolls (page 91).

Makes *2 dozen* · **Hands-on** *50 min.* · **Total** *2 hours, 40 min., plus 8 hours chill time*

1 cup boiling water
³/₄ cup unsalted butter, melted and divided
2 (¹/₄-oz.) envelopes active dry yeast
¹/₂ cup warm water (100° to 110°F)

¹/₂ cup plus 1 tsp. sugar, divided
2 large eggs, lightly beaten
2 tsp. table salt
6 cups all-purpose flour

1. Pour boiling water over ¹/₂ cup butter in bowl of a heavy-duty electric stand mixer, and stir until combined. Let stand 10 minutes or until about 110°F.
2. Meanwhile, combine yeast, warm water, and 1 tsp. sugar in a 1-cup liquid measuring cup; let stand 5 minutes.
3. Add yeast mixture and eggs to butter mixture; beat at low speed, using dough hook attachment, until combined. Beat in salt and remaining ¹/₂ cup sugar. Gradually add flour, beating at low speed 2 to 3 minutes or until flour is blended and dough is soft and smooth.
4. Place dough in a lightly greased large bowl, turning to grease top. Cover and chill 8 to 15 hours.
5. Turn dough out onto a lightly floured surface, and knead until smooth and elastic (about 1 minute). Gently shape dough into 72 balls; place 3 dough balls in each cup of 2 lightly greased 12-cup muffin pans. Brush rolls with remaining ¹/₄ cup melted butter.
6. Cover pans with plastic wrap, and let rise in a warm place (80° to 85°F), free from drafts, 1 hour or until doubled in bulk.
7. Preheat oven to 375°F. Bake rolls for 17 to 20 minutes or until golden brown, rotating pans halfway through. Serve immediately.

ICEBOX CINNAMON ROLLS

No Christmas mornings in Texas would be the same for my family without this particularly special treat.

Makes *2 dozen* · **Hands-on** *1 hour, 45 min.* · **Total** *11 hours, 30 min.*

2 (¹/₄-oz.) envelopes active dry yeast
1 ¹/₂ cups warm water (100° to 110°F)
3 ¹/₂ cups plus 1 tsp. granulated sugar, divided
2 large eggs
2 tsp. table salt

1 ¹/₂ cups unsalted butter, melted and divided
6 cups all-purpose flour
3 cups firmly packed brown sugar
2 Tbsp. ground cinnamon
2 (16-oz.) jars orange marmalade

1. Combine yeast, warm water, and 1 tsp. sugar in a 1-cup liquid measuring cup; let stand 5 minutes.
2. Beat eggs at medium speed with a heavy-duty electric stand mixer, using dough hook attachment. Beat in ¹/₂ cup granulated sugar and salt. Add ¹/₂ cup butter and yeast mixture, beating until blended. Gradually add flour, beating at low speed 1 to 2 minutes or until well blended.
3. Turn dough out onto a lightly floured surface, and knead until smooth and elastic (about 1 minute). Place dough in a lightly greased large bowl, turning to grease top. Cover and chill 8 hours or overnight.
4. Combine brown sugar, cinnamon, and remaining 3 cups granulated sugar in a medium bowl. Set aside.
5. Punch dough down; turn out onto a lightly floured surface. Divide dough in half, and cover 1 portion with a damp towel. Roll remaining portion into a 13- x 10-inch rectangle (about ¹/₄ inch thick).
6. Brush dough with 2 ¹/₂ Tbsp. melted butter, and sprinkle with 2 cups cinnamon mixture. Roll up dough, jelly-roll fashion, starting at 1 long side; cut into 12 slices (about 1 inch thick). Repeat with remaining dough.
7. Coat bottom and sides of 2 (13- x 9-inch) pans with ¹/₄ cup melted butter each. Spread 1 jar orange marmalade on bottoms of each pan, and sprinkle each with 1 cup cinnamon mixture. Place rolls, cut sides up, in pans. Cover and let rise in a warm place (80° to 85°F), free from drafts, 1 hour or until doubled in bulk. Brush dough with remaining melted butter.
8. Preheat oven to 350°F. Bake rolls for 35 to 40 minutes or until golden brown. Cool in pans 5 minutes. Invert rolls onto a serving platter; spoon any sauce in pans over top. Serve immediately.

BANANA PUDDING

No soulful Southern meal is complete without a rich and creamy dessert. My all-time favorite is my mom's banana pudding. The key to this dessert is the custard. Don't cheat with banana-flavored versions or boxed vanilla pudding. Homemade makes all the difference.

Makes *8 to 12 servings* · **Hands-on** *25 min.* · **Total** *7 hours, 25 min.*

1 cup sugar
¹/₄ cup cornstarch
1 tsp. table salt
4 cups milk
4 large egg yolks, lightly beaten
2 Tbsp. butter

1 tsp. vanilla extract
¹/₄ tsp. almond extract (optional)
1 ¹/₂ (11-oz.) boxes vanilla wafers
4 to 5 ripe bananas, cut into ¹/₄-inch slices
Sweetened whipped cream (optional)
Garnish: chopped vanilla wafers

1. Whisk together first 3 ingredients in a medium-size heavy saucepan. Gradually whisk in milk, whisking until well blended. Bring to a boil over medium heat, whisking constantly. Boil, whisking constantly, 2 minutes or until thickened. Remove pan from heat.
2. Whisk egg yolks until slightly thick and pale. Gradually whisk about one-fourth of hot milk mixture into yolks. Add yolk mixture to remaining hot milk mixture, whisking constantly. Bring mixture to a light boil. Cook, whisking constantly, 1 minute. Remove from heat, and whisk in butter, vanilla, and, if desired, almond extract.
3. Transfer mixture to a shallow baking dish. Place plastic wrap directly on cream mixture (to prevent a film from forming), and chill 3 to 4 hours.
4. Arrange one-third of vanilla wafers in a single layer on bottom and sides of a 13- x 9-inch baking dish. Top with half of banana slices and half of pudding. Repeat procedure with remaining wafers, banana slices, and pudding. Cover and chill 4 to 24 hours. Top with whipped cream, if desired.

ROYERS BUTTERMILK PIE DELIGHT

In Texas, when you want a good pie, you can't go wrong with a stop at Royers Pie Haven in Round Top. An accidental slipup from one of their bakers sent a few wayward chocolate chips into a standard buttermilk pie. The mishap spurred a new crowd favorite. It's a home run for anyone with a serious sweet tooth.

Makes *8 to 10 servings* · **Hands-on** *15 min.* · **Total** *4 hours, 40 min., including crust and filling*

Piecrust (recipe follows)
1/3 cup chopped toasted pecans
1/3 cup sweetened flaked coconut
1/3 cup semisweet chocolate morsels
1 1/2 cups sugar
1/4 cup all-purpose flour
1/4 tsp. freshly grated nutmeg

3 large eggs
1/2 cup butter, melted and cooled
1 cup buttermilk, at room temperature
2 tsp. vanilla extract
Garnishes: whipped cream, toasted
    coconut, chocolate chips, pecans

1. Preheat oven to 350°F. Combine pecans, coconut, and chocolate morsels in a bowl. Sprinkle half of pecan mixture into Piecrust; set aside.
2. Whisk together sugar and next 2 ingredients in a medium bowl. Whisk in eggs and cooled butter until well blended. Whisk in buttermilk and vanilla. Gently pour filling over top. Sprinkle top with remaining pecan mixture.
3. Bake at 350°F for 48 to 53 minutes or until almost set, shielding edges with aluminum foil after 30 minutes. Transfer to a wire rack, and cool completely (about 2 hours).

PIECRUST

Makes *1 (9-inch) crust* · **Hands-on** *10 min.* · **Total** *40 min.*

1 1/4 cups all-purpose flour
Pinch of table salt

1/2 cup cold unsalted butter, cubed
1/4 cup ice water

1. Pulse flour and salt in a food processor 3 or 4 times or until combined. Add butter; pulse until mixture resembles small peas. Drizzle ice water over mixture; pulse until dough clumps together. Shape dough into a flat disk. Wrap in plastic wrap, and chill 30 minutes.
2. Preheat oven to 425°F. Roll dough into a 12-inch circle on a lightly floured surface. Fit into a 9-inch pie plate; crimp edges. Line dough with aluminum foil, and fill with pie weights or dried beans.
3. Bake at 425°F for 15 minutes. Remove weights and foil, and bake 10 more minutes or until lightly browned. Transfer to a wire rack, and cool completely (about 30 minutes).

TEXAS TIDBIT

BUTTERMILK

Before baking powder entered the scene, an acid was required to release the carbon dioxide that forced the dough or batter to rise. In Texas, that chemical catalyst was buttermilk. Today it's still used as a baking ingredient for biscuits, German Chocolate Cake, and Texas Sheet Cake, to name a few.

FRENCH APPLE PIE

Another favorite pie for the holidays, my aunt's French Apple Pie is a recipe she's been whipping up for more than 30 years. The filling in this pie bakes to an applesauce-like consistency. It may bubble over the edges while baking, so place a sheet of aluminum foil on the bottom of the oven to catch any drips. Don't place the pie on a baking sheet. The pie plate will stick to it because of the sugary filling. Serve with vanilla ice cream.

Makes *8 to 10 servings* · **Hands-on** *30 min.* · **Total** *2 hours, 20 min.*

1 1/4 cups plus 3 Tbsp. all-purpose flour, divided
1/4 tsp. plus a pinch of table salt, divided
1/2 cup cold unsalted butter, cubed
1/4 cup ice water
3 to 3 1/2 lb. Granny Smith apples, peeled and thinly sliced
2/3 cup sugar

1 tsp. ground cinnamon
2 tsp. fresh lemon juice

CRUMBLE TOPPING
1 cup all-purpose flour
2/3 cup firmly packed brown sugar
1/2 cup cold unsalted butter, cubed

1. Preheat oven to 400°F. Pulse 1 1/4 cups flour and a pinch of table salt in a food processor 3 or 4 times or until combined. Add butter, and pulse 8 to 10 times or until mixture resembles small peas. Drizzle ice water over mixture; pulse until dough clumps together. Gently shape dough into a flat disk. Wrap in plastic wrap, and chill 30 minutes.
2. Preheat oven to 400°F. Roll dough into a 12-inch circle (about 1/8 inch thick) on a floured surface. Fit into a 9-inch pie plate; crimp edges. Refrigerate until ready to fill.
3. Combine apples, sugar, cinnamon, lemon juice, and remaining 3 Tbsp. flour and 1/4 tsp. salt. Let stand 15 minutes, stirring occasionally.
4. Prepare the Crumble Topping: Combine flour and brown sugar in a bowl. Cut in butter with pastry blender or fork until mixture resembles small peas.
5. Spoon fruit mixture into crust; sprinkle top with Crumble Topping.
6. Bake at 400°F for 20 to 25 minutes or until lightly browned. Reduce oven temperature to 350°F. Bake at 350°F for 1 hour or until topping is golden brown and apples are soft and tender when pierced with a wooden pick, shielding with aluminum foil to prevent excessive browning. Serve warm with vanilla ice cream.

TEXAS PECAN PIE

If you ask my grandfather, no Thanksgiving or Christmas was complete without a pecan pie baked by my aunt. It wasn't just the contents of the pie that tasted so good, it was the crust. She was one of the few people who took the time to make a homemade crust. Her method is about patience and restraint. Don't fight the dough and don't overwork it. Simply get it to come together and get it in the pie dish as quickly as you can.

Makes *8 to 10 servings* · **Hands-on** *15 min.* · **Total** *4 hours, not including pie dough*

Piecrust (page 95)
³/₄ cup firmly packed brown sugar
³/₄ cup light corn syrup
¹/₄ cup butter, melted
1 tsp. white vinegar

1 tsp. vanilla extract
¹/₄ tsp. table salt
3 large eggs, lightly beaten
1 ¹/₄ cups pecan halves

1. Preheat oven to 425°F. Prepare Piecrust. Roll out dough into a 12-inch circle on a lightly floured surface. Place in a 9-inch pie plate; fold edges under, and crimp. Line dough with aluminum foil; fill with pie weights or dried beans.
2. Bake at 425°F for 15 minutes or until crust is set. Remove pie weights and foil; bake 10 more minutes or until crust is lightly golden. Cool on a wire rack 30 minutes.
3. Reduce oven temperature to 350°F. Whisk together brown sugar and next 6 ingredients. Pour into cooled crust. Arrange pecans on top of filling.
4. Bake at 350°F for 45 to 50 minutes or until golden brown and center is almost set, shielding edges with foil during last 15 minutes of baking to prevent excessive browning, if necessary. Cool completely on a wire rack (about 2 hours).

NEIMAN MARCUS CAKE

This rich dessert has the texture of a brownie with traditional German chocolate cake ingredients and a sweet cream cheese topping. Many know the story about a famous Neiman Marcus cookie recipe that was once purchased for $250, but this recipe from the Texas flagship store seems to have flown under the radar. Some use yellow cake batter as the base, but I think the German chocolate is much better.

Makes *6 to 8 servings* · **Hands-on** *20 min.* · **Total** *2 hours*

1 (4-oz.) unsweetened chocolate baking bar, chopped
$^3/_4$ cup butter, cut into pieces
2 cups granulated sugar
4 large eggs
$^1/_2$ cup milk

2 tsp. vanilla extract, divided
2 $^1/_4$ cups all-purpose flour
1 tsp. baking soda
$^1/_2$ tsp. table salt
1 (8-oz.) package cream cheese, softened
2 cups powdered sugar

1. Preheat oven to 350°F. Microwave chocolate and butter in a large microwave-safe bowl at HIGH 1 $^1/_2$ to 2 minutes or until melted and smooth, stirring at 30-second intervals. Whisk in granulated sugar. Add 2 eggs, 1 at a time, whisking just until blended after each addition. Whisk in milk and 1 tsp. vanilla.
2. Combine flour, baking soda, and salt in a bowl. Gradually add flour mixture to chocolate mixture, whisking until blended. Pour batter into a greased 13- x 9-inch baking pan. (Batter will be thick.)
3. Beat cream cheese and remaining 1 tsp. vanilla at medium speed with an electric mixer until creamy. Gradually add powdered sugar, beating well. Add remaining 2 eggs, 1 at a time, beating just until yellow disappears after each addition. Pour mixture over chocolate mixture, and spread evenly, being careful not to mix layers.
4. Bake at 350°F for 40 minutes or until a wooden pick inserted in center comes out with a few moist crumbs. Cool completely on a wire rack (about 1 hour).

CHAPTER THREE

COASTAL
★ TEXAS ★

During the mid-19th century, Galveston emerged as an international city and one of the biggest cities in the state for immigration and trade. The island was once considered the "Ellis Island of the West" as the primary point of entry for European immigrants settling in the western United States. Over time, fishing towns eager to harness the freshest catch of the Gulf's bountiful waters popped up along the entire Texas coastline from Beaumont to Corpus Christi and Brownsville.

CEVICHE

Chef Lou Lambert makes ceviche by poaching the seafood just slightly before adding any remaining ingredients instead of only letting the fish "cook" from the acid of lime juice and alcohol from either beer or tequila. The key to great ceviche is to wait to add all of the fresh vegetables and herbs until just before serving. Otherwise, the vegetables can become mushy and overpower the flavors.

Makes *6 servings* · **Hands-on** *20 min.* · **Total** *2 hours, 40 min.*

³/₄ lb. unpeeled, large raw shrimp, peeled and deveined
¹/₂ lb. mild white fish (such as mahi-mahi or red fish)
2 bay leaves
¹/₄ cup fresh lemon juice (1 large lemon)
2 Tbsp. table salt
¹/₄ cup plus 1 ¹/₂ Tbsp. fresh lime juice (3 limes), divided

2 Tbsp. white tequila
3 plum tomatoes, seeded and diced
1 jalapeño pepper, finely chopped
3 green onions, chopped
¹/₃ cup chopped fresh cilantro
¹/₄ cup finely chopped red onion
Thick tortilla chips

1. Cut shrimp and fish into bite-size chunks.
2. Bring 6 cups water, bay leaves, lemon juice, and salt to a boil in a medium saucepan over medium heat. Reduce heat, and add shrimp; simmer 30 seconds or just until shrimp turn pink. Drain, discarding liquid and bay leaves. Let cool completely (about 15 minutes).
3. Combine fish, shrimp, ¹/₄ cup lime juice, and tequila in a large zip-top plastic freezer bag. Seal and chill 2 hours, turning occasionally.
4. Transfer seafood mixture to a serving bowl. Stir in tomatoes and next 4 ingredients. Stir in remaining 1 ¹/₂ Tbsp. lime juice and salt to taste. Serve cold with thick tortilla chips.

LONGHORN GREEN SALAD

One of the highlights of the Taste of Texas restaurant in Houston is the lush salad bar, piled high with greens, carrots, garlicky croutons, ripe tomatoes, and a Texas-sized block of longhorn-style Cheddar cheese waiting at the end for shaving into silky ribbons to adorn your salad. A generous helping of Ranch dressing is perfect here. This is a take on that salad I remember from my childhood.

Makes *8 servings* · **Hands-on** *15 min.* · **Total** *15 min.*

1 large head red leaf lettuce, torn
    (about 10 cups)
1 pt. grape tomatoes
1 cup thinly sliced red onion
1 ¹/₂ cups (6 oz.) shredded longhorn-style
    Cheddar cheese*

¹/₂ cup Cilantro Ranch Dressing
    (recipe follows)
Cornbread Croutons (page 88)

Toss together first 4 ingredients in a large bowl. Drizzle with Cilantro Ranch Dressing; toss gently. Divide salad mixture among serving plates; top with Cornbread Croutons.

*Mild Cheddar cheese may be substituted for longhorn-style Cheddar cheese.

CILANTRO RANCH DRESSING

Makes *1 cup* · **Hands-on** *10 min.* · **Total** *40 min.*

¹/₂ cup buttermilk
¹/₂ cup mayonnaise
3 Tbsp. chopped fresh cilantro
2 tsp. firmly packed lemon zest

¹/₄ tsp. table salt
¹/₄ tsp. freshly ground black pepper
1 small garlic clove, minced
1 green onion, finely chopped

Combine all ingredients in a 1-qt. glass jar with a tight-fitting lid. Cover and shake vigorously to blend. Chill 30 minutes. Refrigerate in covered jar up to 1 week. Shake well before serving.

TOMATO, AVOCADO, AND COTIJA SALAD

This is a great way to enjoy the fresh flavors of classic guacamole in crunchy salad form. Try it atop grilled fish tacos too.

Makes *4 to 6 servings* · **Hands-on** *20 min.* · **Total** *45 min.*

TEXAS TIDBIT

HOUSTON RODEO TRAIL RIDES

Each year, more than a dozen trail rides begin from all directions to converge at the Houston Rodeo Parade that marches through downtown Houston. The first trail ride began in 1952 as the Salt Grass Trail ride from Brenham, whose mayor, Reese Lockett, announced that the only way he would arrive at a rodeo was on horseback. Since then 12 more official trail rides have formed from the Los Vaqueros Rio Grande Trail Ride from Hidalgo 386 miles away to the Old Spanish Trail Ride from Logansport, Louisiana, 216 miles away.

5 plum tomatoes, quartered
$\frac{1}{2}$ tsp. table salt
2 ripe avocados, cubed
$\frac{1}{2}$ cup chopped fresh cilantro
1 jalapeño pepper, seeded and finely chopped

1 garlic clove, pressed
2 Tbsp. extra virgin olive oil
1 Tbsp. fresh lime juice
$\frac{1}{2}$ tsp. freshly ground black pepper
$\frac{1}{2}$ cup crumbled Cotija cheese*

1. Toss together tomatoes and salt; drain on a paper towel-lined baking sheet 15 minutes.
2. Combine tomatoes, avocados, and next 6 ingredients in a large bowl. Let stand 10 to 15 minutes. Sprinkle with cheese, and serve immediately.

*Feta cheese may be substituted for Cotija cheese.

CHRIS SHEPHERD

CHEF/RESTAURATEUR, UNDERBELLY, HAY MERCHANT, HOUSTON

Chris Shepherd has the physique of a star running back or bronc-busting rodeo celebrity, yet he chose to make his mark cooking.

The Tulsa native went to culinary school at the Art Institute of Houston where he quickly found a foothold for his career. He recalls a visit to the coast when he watched the fishing boats unload their catch, and he was hooked.

"That's not something I could do in Tulsa," says Shepherd. "Seeing these varieties of species that come from the Gulf was amazing. It's what kept me in Texas."

Shepherd spent time in a few iconic Houston restaurants as a sous chef and sommelier at Brennan's of Houston and as the executive chef at Spanish-inspired Catalan. Seeking a new way to use food as a statement, Shepherd left Catalan to develop his own restaurant concept that would borrow from the flavors of Houston's diverse immigrant population and reveal a formal identity of flavor for the city.

He took time to apprentice at other restaurants throughout town, but instead of looking to high-end, big-name restaurants, he deliberately sought out places that could give him an authentic edge on the true heart of Houston cooking. They included places like Asia Market, London Sizzler Indian Bar & Grill, Thanh Phuong, and Mala Sichuan Bistro. He learned how to cook Korean food as well.

In 2012, he debuted Underbelly, drawing immediate national acclaim and garnering Shepherd a James Beard Award for Best Chef: Southwest. Drawing from the cultures that make up the fabric of Houston including Mexican, Southern Cajun, French, Vietnamese, Thai, Korean, Indian, German, and Texan, the menu, which changes daily, is a tribute to the city itself. On it you'll find a wide variety of dishes, from German schnitzel or Korean braised goat and rice dumplings to wild boar porchetta with grits or Thai-style red curry pork and noodles.

The restaurant is more than just a patchwork menu of cultures, it's a statement about responsibility. Where ingredients come from and how they're treated once they arrive at the restaurant's back door is critical to Shepherd. Underbelly's kitchen has a full-scale butcher shop where whole animals from area ranches are processed, using every possible inch of the animal.

"Underbelly is really about revealing a side of things not seen," he says. "We highlight the great cultural diversity this city has but also the local farming, ranching, and Gulf waters that a lot of people don't even pay attention to. Just as many different ethnicities beyond Mexican and American make up the flavors of this part of Texas, the food in this part of the state is only as good as the sum of its parts, and altogether, it's some really good stuff."

"Just as many different ethnicities beyond Mexican and American make up the flavors of this part of Texas, the food . . . is only as good as the sum of its parts, and altogether, it's some really good stuff."

CRISPY POPCORN SHRIMP WITH BUTTERED CORN DIPPING SAUCE

Houston Chef Chris Shepherd is one of many Gulf Coast area chefs who have garnered a reputation for taking the best of the Gulf's catch. And when it comes to shrimp, there's no better place to get it. These savory little popcorn bites are an addictive treat either as an appetizer or main dish.

Makes *6 to 8 appetizer servings* · **Hands-on** *45 min.* · **Total** *2 hours*

TEXAS TOOLS

Corn Husks

Beyond protecting the corn cob inside, the thick, paper-like corn husk is an essential tool for shaping, holding, and steaming traditional tamales. They are available dried in Mexican markets, but when corn is in season and you're making recipes like this one, don't discard the husks after shucking. Dry them directly on the racks in your oven set to the lowest temperature (about 140°F) for 8 hours, leaving the door slightly ajar. Let them cool and store in an airtight container.

4 ears fresh corn, husked
1 onion, quartered
1 garlic clove, crushed
1/2 cup heavy cream
1 cup cold butter, cut into 16 pieces
1/2 tsp. kosher salt
2 cups rice flour
1 cup milk
2 large eggs
1 lb. peeled and deveined, small raw shrimp
Vegetable oil

1. Cut kernels from corn; reserve kernels and cobs.
2. Combine cobs, onion, garlic, and 4 cups water in a large saucepan. Bring to a boil over medium-high heat. Reduce heat to medium, and simmer, stirring occasionally, 40 minutes or until liquid is reduced to 3/4 cup. Pour mixture through a wire-mesh strainer into a bowl, discarding solids.
3. Return broth to saucepan. Add reserved corn kernels and heavy cream. Bring to a boil over medium-high heat; reduce heat to medium, and simmer 5 minutes or until liquid is slightly reduced. Cover, reduce heat to low, and simmer 7 minutes or until corn is tender. Cool slightly.
4. Puree the corn mixture, in batches, in a blender. Wipe saucepan clean. Pour mixture through a wire-mesh strainer into saucepan, discarding solids. Cook over low heat. Add butter, 1 piece at a time, whisking constantly until butter is melted. Whisk in kosher salt; cover and keep warm.
5. Place flour in a shallow dish. Whisk together milk and eggs in another dish. Dredge shrimp, in batches, in flour, shaking off excess; dip in egg mixture, and in flour, shaking off excess.
6. Pour oil to depth of 1 1/2 inches into a Dutch oven; heat to 350°F. Fry shrimp, in batches, 1 to 2 minutes on each side or until golden. Drain on wire racks over paper towels; sprinkle with salt and freshly ground black pepper to taste. Serve with warm corn sauce.

CRAB CAKES WITH LEMON BUTTER

Avoid compressing the cakes to keep the lumps of Gulf crab meat large and plump for best results.

Makes *12 servings* · **Hands-on** *45 min.* · **Total** *1 hour, 30 min., not including butter*

1/2 cup finely diced red bell pepper
1/2 cup finely diced green bell pepper
1/2 cup finely diced yellow onion
2 Tbsp. minced garlic
1/2 cup olive oil, divided
2 Tbsp. Creole or Dijon mustard
2 Tbsp. Worcestershire sauce
1 tsp. kosher salt
1/2 tsp. freshly ground black pepper

1/8 tsp. ground red pepper
3/4 cup fine, dry breadcrumbs
2 large eggs, lightly beaten
1 1/2 lb. fresh lump crabmeat, picked and drained
1/2 cup finely chopped green onions
3 Tbsp. butter
Lemon Butter (recipe follows)
Garnish: fresh flat-leaf parsley

1. Sauté bell peppers, onion, and garlic in 2 Tbsp. hot oil over medium-high heat 8 to 10 minutes. Stir in mustard and next 4 ingredients. Add breadcrumbs, and sauté 1 minute. Transfer mixture to a large bowl. Cool 15 minutes.
2. Fold eggs into bread crumb mixture until blended. Gently stir in crabmeat and green onions. Shape into 15 (3-inch) cakes (about 1/3 cup each). Chill 30 to 40 minutes.
3. Melt 1 Tbsp. butter with 2 Tbsp. oil in a large nonstick skillet over medium heat. Add 4 crab cakes to skillet; cook 3 to 4 minutes on each side or until browned. Remove from skillet, and keep warm. Repeat procedure with remaining oil, butter, and crab cakes, wiping skillet clean after each use. Serve with Lemon Butter.

LEMON BUTTER

Makes *2 cups* · **Hands-on** *20 min.* · **Total** *20 min.*

1 lemon, peeled and quartered
1 shallot, minced
1/4 cup dry white wine
1 bay leaf

1 1/2 tsp. black peppercorns
2 cups unsalted butter, cut into pieces
1/2 tsp. table salt
Pinch of ground white pepper

1. Bring first 5 ingredients to a simmer in a heavy saucepan over medium heat. Cook until liquid almost completely evaporates. Reduce heat to low and whisk in butter, 1 piece at a time, whisking constantly and allowing butter to melt between each addition.
2. Pour mixture through a wire-mesh strainer into a bowl, discarding solids. Stir in salt and pepper. Keep warm until ready to serve.

TEXAS GULF FISH TACOS

My dad takes the reds and trout he catches in the shallow flats of the bay of Port O'Connor to Josie's Mexican Food restaurant where they cook them up with spices and serve in fresh homemade tortillas. I like to add slaw and spicy mayo for contrast.

Makes *4 to 6 servings* · **Hands-on** *25 min.* · **Total** *50 min., including slaw and mayo*

2 Tbsp. white wine vinegar
2 tsp. canola oil
¹/₂ tsp. table salt
¹/₄ tsp. freshly ground black pepper
4 cups shredded cabbage
¹/₂ cup chopped fresh cilantro
4 green onions, chopped
Vegetable cooking spray
4 (6-oz.) skinless mahi-mahi fillets
2 tsp. canola oil

2 tsp. ancho chile powder
¹/₂ tsp. table salt
¹/₂ tsp. freshly ground black pepper
¹/₄ tsp. dried Mexican oregano
¹/₄ tsp. ground cumin
12 corn tortillas
Spicy Chipotle Mayo (recipe follows)
Lime wedges
Garnish: fresh cilantro

1. Whisk together vinegar and next 3 ingredients in a large bowl. Add cabbage, cilantro, and green onions; toss to coat. Cover and chill slaw until ready to assemble tacos.
2. Coat cold cooking grate with cooking spray, and place on grill. Preheat grill to 350° to 400°F (medium-high) heat. Rub both sides of fish with oil.
3. Stir together ancho chile powder and next 4 ingredients; rub chile powder mixture evenly over both sides of fish, pressing to adhere.
4. Grill fish, covered with grill lid, 4 to 5 minutes on each side. Remove and cover with foil; keep warm.
5. Grill tortillas, in batches, 10 to 20 seconds on each side, and wrap in aluminum foil.
6. Flake fish into bite-size pieces, and serve in grilled tortillas with slaw, Spicy Chipotle Mayo, and lime wedges.

SPICY CHIPOTLE MAYO

Makes *³/₄ cup* · **Hands-on** *10 min.* · **Total** *10 min.*

³/₄ cup mayonnaise
1 Tbsp. minced canned chipotle pepper in adobo sauce

1 Tbsp. fresh lime juice
1 garlic clove, minced

Stir together all ingredients. Cover and chill until ready to serve. Refrigerate in an airtight container up to 1 week.

OYSTERS WITH TWO BUTTERS

Jack Gilmore's method of grilling Texas Gulf oysters with a duo of flavored butters is pretty spectacular. Smoke from the grill adds a nice dimension to the oysters' brininess. Caution when handling these: Don't douse yourself with the hot melted butter.

Makes *10 to 12 servings* · **Hands-on** *20 min.* · **Total** *4 hours, 45 min., including butters*

2 dozen large fresh oysters on the half shell

BACON AND CAYENNE BUTTER
2 bacon slices, cut into 1/2-inch pieces
1/2 cup unsalted butter, softened
1 Tbsp. chopped fresh flat-leaf parsley
1 Tbsp. chopped fresh cilantro
1 Tbsp. chopped garlic
2 Tbsp. pale ale beer, such as Peacemaker
    Extra Pale Ale
1 Tbsp. fresh lemon juice
1/2 tsp. kosher salt

1/2 tsp. freshly ground black pepper
1/4 tsp. ground red pepper
Dash of Worcestershire sauce

CHIPOTLE BUTTER
2 Tbsp. bourbon
1 tsp. brown sugar
1/2 cup unsalted butter, softened
1 Tbsp. fresh lime juice
1 Tbsp. chopped garlic
2 canned chipotle peppers in adobo sauce

1. Prepare the Bacon and Cayenne Butter: Cook bacon in a medium skillet over medium heat, stirring often, 6 to 8 minutes or until crisp; remove bacon, and drain on paper towels, discarding drippings in skillet. Cool 5 minutes.
2. Process bacon, butter, and next 6 ingredients in a food processor until smooth, stopping to scrape down sides as needed. Cover and chill 4 to 6 hours.
3. Prepare the Chipotle Butter: Combine bourbon and brown sugar in a medium bowl, stirring until sugar dissolves.
4. Process bourbon mixture, butter, and remaining ingredients in a food processor until smooth, stopping to scrape down sides as needed. Cover and chill 4 to 6 hours. (Butters may be shaped into logs with plastic wrap, and frozen up to 1 month.)
5. Preheat grill to 450°F (high) heat. Arrange oysters in a single layer on grill. Spoon 2 tsp. Bacon and Cayenne Butter or Chipotle Butter into each oyster; grill, without grill lid, 7 minutes or until edges curl. Serve immediately.

TEXAS PIT STOPS

KING'S INN
Baffin Bay

GAIDO'S
Galveston

JAMES CONEY ISLAND
Houston

REVIVAL MARKET
Houston

NINFA'S ON NAVIGATION
Houston

TONY'S
Houston

SARTIN'S SEAFOOD
Nederland

GLOW
Rockport

GRILLED REDFISH WITH CILANTRO-SERRANO CHIMICHURRI

Fishing for redfish in the flats along the Gulf Coast is a spiritual experience for most Texas anglers. There's something about taking a trip down to the bay and bringing home a cooler of fresh fish to cook on the grill. Any mild flaky fish works well in this recipe, and the chimichurri is the perfect sauce to bring out the natural flavor.

Makes *4 servings* · **Hands-on** *20 min.* · **Total** *30 min.*

1 (1 1/4-lb.) skinless redfish fillet
Vegetable cooking spray
1 tsp. table salt, divided
1 tsp. freshly ground black pepper, divided
Juice of 1/2 lemon
1 cup chopped fresh cilantro
1/2 cup extra virgin olive oil

2 serrano peppers, seeded and coarsely chopped
5 green onions, coarsely chopped
3 garlic cloves, coarsely chopped
2 Tbsp. fresh lime juice
Green Rice (page 192)
Garnish: fresh cilantro

1. Preheat grill to 400° to 450°F (high) heat. Coat fish lightly with cooking spray; sprinkle with 1/2 tsp. salt, 1/2 tsp. pepper, and lemon juice.
2. Process cilantro, remaining salt and pepper, olive oil, and next 4 ingredients in a food processor until slightly chunky.
3. Place fish on grill rack coated with cooking spray. Grill fish, covered with grill lid, 6 minutes on each side or until fish flakes with a fork. Serve over Green Rice with sauce.

TEXAS TOOLS

Charcoal Starter Chimney

Gone are the days when you had to build a charcoal briquette pyramid and spray it down with lighter fluid to start a fire on the grill. These days the task is much more efficiently managed with a metal chimney-shaped device that allows you to put charcoal in the top side and a stash of paper on the bottom side. With a single light of a match, you've got a lit fire that will yield perfectly hot coals in about 20 minutes and infuse whatever you're grilling with flavor that's difficult to achieve with a gas grill.

JACK GILMORE

CHEF/OWNER OF JACK ALLEN'S KITCHEN, AUSTIN

If there's anything that brings peace and inspiration to Jack Gilmore, it's the Texas coast. In some ways, it's because of the rhythmic swells the tides bring in and out and the abundance of seafood flourishing in this marine oasis. While Gilmore's restaurant is in the Central part of the state, the Texas coast is home.

Growing up in Brownsville at the southern tip of the coastline near Mexico, Gilmore was influenced by a confluence of Mexican and coastal culture.

"The ocean was a part of our lives growing up. My friends' dads would fish the surf and give us chicken necks to put in crabbing baskets while we were on the shore as kids," says Gilmore who also remembers a time when he worked on a friend's shrimping boat. "That was an awakening for me about just how hard that life is. We were on this big, old wooden boat with manual cranks on the fishing gear. We'd work at night and sleep during the day. When the nets came in, you'd pray it was full of shrimp and not by-catch."

Though he spent only one season on the boat, he saw enough to appreciate the hard work that goes into it. Decades later, having built his career as a chef in Central Texas at iconic Austin restaurants Chez Fred and Z Tejas, Gilmore is now the owner of his own three-location concept, Jack Allen's Kitchen. Serving up seasonal Texas-inspired fare, he still looks to the coast for inspiration.

"A lot of people take for granted what a fantastic resource that's literally in our own backyard," says Gilmore. "With the exception of salmon and ruby red trout, all of our fish comes from the Gulf at my restaurants."

In 2012, he placed third in the Great American Seafood Cook-off in New Orleans against 15 other national chefs using Texas brown shrimp as his featured ingredient. To this day, when he's sourcing shrimp for his restaurants, if it's not from the Gulf, he won't buy it.

"The Gulf fishermen work really hard to bring in some of the best-tasting shrimp you'll find anywhere in the world," says Gilmore, who also loves Texas oysters. "The Galveston Bay is one of the best oyster fisheries in the country," says Gilmore. "They're briny and creamy and taste like the sea. It's my favorite time of year when they're in season."

Today, Gilmore doesn't let more than a couple of months slip by without escaping to the coast for a few days of fishing.

"If a few months go by and I haven't been fishing, I start to get antsy," says Gilmore. "It's where I can really unwind. It's a vacation and going back to my roots at the same time, and that's what helps me stay focused on doing my job every day."

"A lot of people take for granted what a fantastic resource that's literally in our own backyard. With the exception of salmon and ruby red trout, all of our fish comes from the Gulf at my restaurants."

SHRIMP CREOLE

Chef Jack Gilmore highlights local seafood on his menus to pay homage to his coastal roots. Spoon this over Pimiento Cheese Grits (page 64) for a kicked-up version of classic shrimp and grits.

Makes *8 servings* · **Hands-on** *1 hour, 10 min.* · **Total** *1 hour, 20 min., including seasoning*

3 lb. unpeeled, large raw shrimp, peeled
    and deveined
2 to 3 Tbsp. Shrimp Seasoning
    (recipe follows)
6 Tbsp. butter, softened and divided
2 cups chopped onion
1 cup chopped green bell pepper
1 cup chopped celery
3 garlic cloves, minced

1 tsp. table salt
1 (28-oz.) can diced tomatoes
2 bay leaves
1 Tbsp. Worcestershire sauce
Hot sauce
2 Tbsp. all-purpose flour
Garnishes: chopped green onions,
    chopped fresh parsley

1. Sprinkle shrimp with Shrimp Seasoning; set aside.
2. Melt 1/4 cup butter in a Dutch oven over medium heat. Add next 5 ingredients; sauté 20 minutes or until vegetables are tender and lightly caramelized.
3. Stir in tomatoes, bay leaves, and 2 1/2 cups water. Bring to a boil over medium-high heat; reduce heat to medium-low, and simmer, uncovered and stirring occasionally, 15 minutes. Add Worcestershire sauce and hot sauce to taste.
4. Whisk together flour and remaining 2 Tbsp. butter. Add to tomato mixture, whisking until blended. Cook over medium heat 3 minutes or until thickened.
5. Add shrimp, and cook 5 minutes or just until shrimp turn pink. Remove and discard bay leaves before serving.

SHRIMP SEASONING

Makes *1/2 cup* · **Hands-on** *5 min.* · **Total** *5 min.*

2 Tbsp. kosher salt
2 Tbsp. garlic powder
1 Tbsp. onion powder
1 Tbsp. freshly ground black pepper

1 Tbsp. ground red pepper
1 Tbsp. dried oregano
1 Tbsp. dried thyme

Stir together all ingredients until well blended. Store in an airtight container up to 6 months.

JAMBALAYA

The border between Lake Charles and Beaumont feels uncannily similar to the Louisiana bayou region and the foods share a similarity too. Jambalaya is a soulful dish that always includes rice, Cajun-Creole spices, and the holy trinity of vegetables: onions, bell peppers, and celery. Here, the rice soaks up rich flavor while it simmers with the other ingredients.

Makes *10 to 12 servings* · **Hands-on** *1 hour* · **Total** *1 hour, 40 min.*

1 lb. andouille sausage, cut into
    $1/2$-inch slices
2 Tbsp. olive oil
2 red bell peppers, diced
1 green bell pepper, diced
1 onion, diced
3 celery ribs, diced
3 garlic cloves, minced
2 bay leaves
1 tsp. table salt
1 tsp. dried thyme

$1/2$ tsp. ground white pepper
$1/2$ tsp. freshly ground black pepper
$1/2$ tsp. filé powder
$1/4$ tsp. ground red pepper
$2 1/2$ cups uncooked long-grain rice
5 cups chicken broth
1 (28-oz.) can whole tomatoes, drained
    and crushed
$1 1/4$ lb. unpeeled, medium-size raw shrimp,
    peeled and deveined
1 cup sliced green onions

1. Preheat oven to 350°F. Cook sausage in hot oil in a Dutch oven over medium-high heat, stirring constantly, 7 minutes or until browned. Remove sausage with a slotted spoon, and drain on paper towels, reserving drippings in Dutch oven.

2. Add red bell peppers and next 3 ingredients to hot drippings; sauté 10 minutes or until vegetables are tender and lightly browned. Add garlic, and sauté 2 minutes. Add bay leaves and next 6 ingredients, and cook over medium-low heat 5 minutes. Add rice, and cook, stirring constantly, 5 minutes. Add broth and tomatoes, stirring to loosen browned bits from bottom of Dutch oven.

3. Bring to a boil over high heat. Stir in sausage, shrimp, and green onions.

4. Bake, covered, at 350°F for 30 minutes. Let stand 5 minutes. Remove and discard bay leaves before serving.

TEXAS TIDBIT

CAJUN INVASION

Along the coast, Jefferson County, which lies on the state's eastern border with Louisiana, is rooted in Cajun culture. A second wave of Western Louisianans brought more Cajun culture when they crossed into Texas in the 1950s to move closer to oil refinery centers in Beaumont, Port Arthur, and Orange. Moving west along the coastal bend, Galveston Bay is known as one of the country's great natural oyster fisheries, cultivating a great variety of bay- and inlet-specific oysters, each with their own unique flavor.

ANDOUILLE SAUSAGE AND SMOKED CHICKEN GUMBO

With a last name like Dupuy, there's really no excuse for not knowing how to make a good gumbo. Though it's a family I married into, it was almost a rite of passage to get this recipe right. There's no mystery to making a roux, you just have to be brave enough to take it to the point of almost burning before it's just right. Patience is key, and instincts are crucial. And if you burn it the first time, don't worry. You can always try it again.

Makes *6 servings* · **Hands-on** *1 hour* · **Total** *1 hour, 40 min., plus chicken*

$^2/_3$ cup butter, divided
$^1/_2$ lb. andouille sausage, halved lengthwise
  and cut into $^1/_4$-inch-thick slices
$^3/_4$ cup all-purpose flour
1 green bell pepper, finely chopped
1 large onion, finely chopped
3 celery ribs, finely chopped
4 garlic cloves, minced
1 tsp. table salt

1 tsp. freshly ground black pepper
4 cups chicken broth
1 (14.5-oz.) can diced tomatoes
1 tsp. dried oregano
1 tsp. dried thyme
2 bay leaves
2 $^1/_2$ cups shredded Smoked Chicken
  (page 223)
Garnish: sliced green onions

1. Melt 1 Tbsp. butter in a Dutch oven over medium heat. Cook sausage 6 minutes or until browned; remove sausage with a slotted spoon, and drain on paper towels, reserving drippings in Dutch oven. Add remaining butter to Dutch oven. Gradually whisk in flour; cook, whisking constantly, until flour is a milk chocolate color (about 25 minutes).
2. Stir in bell pepper and next 5 ingredients; cook, stirring constantly, 15 minutes or until vegetables are tender. Gradually add broth, stirring until combined. Add tomatoes, oregano, thyme, and bay leaves. Bring to a light boil; reduce heat to low, and simmer, stirring occasionally, 30 minutes or until slightly thickened.
3. Return sausage to pan; simmer, stirring occasionally, 15 minutes. Stir in chicken. Remove and discard bay leaves before serving.

Note: Substitute smoked chicken from your favorite barbecue restaurant, or use shredded deli rotisserie chicken for the Smoked Chicken.

SHRIMP AND OKRA GUMBO

The history of gumbo offers a wide variation of styles and ingredients. This is the version my grandmother in Houston always made using fresh Gulf shrimp and a whole lot of okra. Because it doesn't have a roux, many may contend that it isn't true gumbo. I'm not one to argue with my elders, so I'm sticking to what my grandmother calls this. But if you'd like to call it shrimp and okra stew, you're free to do so.

Makes *12 servings* · **Hands-on** *55 min.* · **Total** *1 hour, 30 min.*

6 Tbsp. butter
2 cups finely chopped onion
1 1/2 cups finely chopped green bell pepper
1 1/2 cups finely chopped celery
5 garlic cloves, minced
1 1/2 tsp. dried thyme
1 1/2 tsp. table salt
1 tsp. freshly ground black pepper
3 (14.5-oz.) cans diced tomatoes

2 (16-oz.) packages frozen cut okra, thawed
1 (32-oz.) container chicken broth
2 bay leaves
2 lb. unpeeled, medium-size raw shrimp, peeled and deveined
1 Tbsp. hot sauce
1 tsp. filé powder
Hot cooked rice

1. Melt butter in a large Dutch oven over medium heat; add onion and next 3 ingredients, and sauté 15 minutes or until vegetables are tender. Stir in thyme, salt, and pepper, and cook 1 to 2 minutes. Stir in tomatoes, okra, broth, and bay leaves.
2. Bring to a boil over medium-high heat; cover, reduce heat to low, and simmer 30 minutes. Add shrimp, hot sauce, and filé powder. Cook 3 to 5 minutes or just until shrimp turn pink. Remove and discard bay leaves. Serve over rice.

TEXAS TIDBIT

TEXAS RICE

Though rice as an agricultural product emerged in the United States more than 200 years ago, it found its hold in Southeast Texas in the 1880s. By the turn of the century it was a full-scale industry with more than 230,000 acres planted. In 1904, a particular Japanese seed was imported near Houston, along with a number of Japanese farmers who taught local farmers their methods of farming. Within the first three years, the harvest was nearly double the yield of previously cultivated rice varieties, making the new style of Japanese rice production the keystone for establishing the Gulf Coast rice industry.

SLOW-BURN BOLOGNESE

Though Italian immigration was fairly minimal in Texas compared to the East Coast, there's no question of the shared love for food cooked low and slow. This is a dish that was passed around by the ladies at my childhood community church. It's Italian-inspired but has a Texas chile pepper kick.

Makes *8 to 10 servings* · **Hands-on** *45 min.* · **Total** *3 hours, 35 min.*

3 fresh thyme sprigs
2 fresh rosemary sprigs
Kitchen string
2 small onions, diced
2 large carrots, diced
3 celery ribs, diced
4 garlic cloves, chopped
1 large jalapeño pepper, seeded and diced
   (optional)
2 1/2 tsp. table salt, divided
3 Tbsp. olive oil

3 lb. ground beef or turkey
2 (6-oz.) cans tomato paste
1 (750-ml.) bottle dry red wine
3 (10-oz.) cans diced tomatoes with
   green chiles
1 (15-oz.) can tomato sauce
3 bay leaves
1 (16-oz.) package spaghetti
Garnishes: freshly grated Parmigiano-
   Reggiano cheese, chopped fresh
   flat-leaf parsley

1. Tie thyme and rosemary together with kitchen string.
2. Process onion, next 3 ingredients, and, if desired, jalapeño pepper in a food processor until mixture resembles a coarse paste, stopping to scrape bowl as needed.
3. Cook vegetable mixture and 2 tsp. salt in hot oil in a large skillet or Dutch oven over medium-high heat, stirring occasionally, 20 to 30 minutes or until vegetables begin to brown.
4. Add ground beef and remaining 1/2 tsp. salt. Brown meat over medium-high heat, stirring often, 10 to 15 minutes or until meat crumbles and is no longer pink.
5. Stir in tomato paste, and cook, stirring occasionally, 4 to 5 minutes or until mixture is a brick-red color. Add red wine, and simmer 10 to 15 minutes or until liquid is reduced by half.
6. Stir in diced tomatoes and tomato sauce. Add bay leaves and herb bundle, and stir gently. Bring to a boil; reduce heat, and simmer, stirring occasionally, 30 minutes. Season with salt to taste. Simmer 2 to 2 1/2 more hours.
7. Meanwhile, prepare pasta according to package directions. Remove and discard bay leaves and herb bundle. Serve sauce over hot cooked pasta.

TEXAS STRIP STEAKS

My first experience at a Texas steakhouse was in Houston at the family-owned Taste of Texas Restaurant, opened by Edd and Nina Hendee in 1977. For years, they've been known for serving up delicious certified Angus steaks and giving guests an ample dose of Texas hospitality and heritage. Buy the highest quality of beef you can afford here. Prime Certified Angus Beef is a great choice.

Makes *4 servings* · **Hands-on** *10 min.* · **Total** *1 hour, 35 min., including rub*

4 (16-oz.) beef strip steaks   4 tsp. Texas Meat Rub (page 13)*
  (1 1/2 inches thick)

1. Sprinkle steaks with Texas Meat Rub, and let stand at room temperature 1 hour.
2. Light 1 side of grill, heating to 400° to 500°F (high) heat; leave other side unlit. Place steaks over lit side, and grill, without grill lid, 2 minutes on each side. Transfer steaks to unlit side. Grill, covered with grill lid, 15 to 20 minutes (medium-rare) or to desired degree of doneness. Remove steaks from grill; let stand 3 minutes before serving.

*2 tsp. salt and 2 tsp. freshly ground black pepper may be substituted for Texas Meat Rub.

TEXAS TIDBIT

THE HOUSTON LIVESTOCK SHOW AND RODEO

Though many Texas towns—large and small— are home to some kind of rodeo, nothing in the state compares to the Houston Livestock Show and Rodeo. A big event for the Space City since 1931, the show has evolved to attract more than 2.5 million people a year during its 20-day celebration of rodeo, livestock, food, wine, entertainment, and all things Texan. Each year, the HLSR is kicked off by the Downtown Rodeo Roundup and the World's Championship Bar-B-Que Contest with 350 teams of smoke-pit competitors cooking up brisket, sausage, ribs, and more.

TEQUILA LIME PIE

This recipe has been a family favorite for years. The best part about it is the crust that caramelizes slightly while baking. Even better, it takes on inspiration from a margarita with the addition of tequila.

Makes *10 to 12 servings* · **Hands-on** *15 min.* · **Total** *2 hours, 40 min., plus chill time*

1 ½ cups graham cracker crumbs
⅓ cup butter, melted
¼ cup firmly packed light brown sugar
3 (14-oz.) cans sweetened condensed milk
5 large egg yolks

1 cup fresh Key lime juice (about 2 lb. Key limes)*
½ cup tequila
Garnishes: sweetened whipped cream, lime slices

1. Preheat oven to 350°F. Stir together first 3 ingredients; firmly press mixture on bottom and up sides of a 9 ½- or 10-inch deep-dish pie plate.
2. Whisk together condensed milk and egg yolks in a large bowl until blended. Gradually whisk in lime juice and tequila until well blended. Pour mixture into crust.
3. Bake at 350°F for 25 minutes or until set around edges. (Pie will be slightly jiggly.) Cool completely on a wire rack (about 2 hours). Cover and chill 8 hours.

*Regular lime juice may be substituted for Key lime juice.

CHAPTER FOUR

SOUTH
★ TEXAS ★

South Texas is the birthplace of Tex-Mex. Long ago, the southern portion of Texas was governed by both Spain and Mexico. It is a region that extends from the Mexico-Laredo border directly northwest to San Antonio, and encompasses the Rio Grande Valley, which is also known as simply The Valley, the Nueces Strip, or the Wild Horse Desert. It is home to a flurry of Mexican-inspired fare, countless orchards of ruby red grapefruit, and the famous King Ranch.

THE ORIGINAL NACHO

Contrary to what many may think, an authentic nacho is a simple tortilla chip topped with a slice of Cheddar cheese and, oftentimes, a slice of fresh or pickled jalapeño. That's it. Rather than a plate of chips that get soggy beneath a mountain of other ingredients, the classic nacho reveals individual chips that remain toasted and crunchy around the outer edges of the gooey, melted cheese.

Makes *4 servings* · **Hands-on** *5 min.* · **Total** *15 min.*

20 tortilla chips
5 sharp Cheddar cheese slices, quartered
   into squares

20 pickled sliced jalapeños
1 (16-oz. can) refried beans (optional)
Garnish: fresh cilantro

1. Preheat oven to 400°F.
2. Arrange tortilla chips in a single layer on large baking sheet. Top each chip with 1 cheese square and 2 jalapeño slices. Top with 1 Tbsp. refried beans, if desired. Bake at 400°F for 5 to 10 minutes or until cheese melts and edges of chips are browned. Serve immediately.

Note: Spread 1 Tbsp. refried beans onto each tortilla chip. Top with 1 cheese slice and 1 jalapeño slice. Bake as directed to turn the Nacho into a Poncho.

TEXAS TOOLS

Comal

A smooth, flat, and round griddle used to cook tortillas, toast spices, and prepare other foods. (They're commonly seen to serve a plate of sizzling fajitas.) Comals are generally made of heavy cast iron, though traditional comals were often made of clay and were slightly concave. A well-seasoned comal is like a well-seasoned cast-iron skillet. It will heat faster and cook cleaner with frequent use.

SIMPLE GUACAMOLE

When it comes to guacamole, the simpler the better. It is great on its own, as a condiment, or served up with tortilla chips. For a twist, add a few spoonfuls of fresh Pico de Gallo (page 153).

Makes *3 cups* · **Hands-on** *10 min.* · **Total** *10 min.*

5 medium-size ripe avocados, halved
2 Tbsp. fresh lime juice
1/2 cup diced red onion
3/4 tsp. kosher salt
1 garlic clove, pressed

Scoop avocado pulp into a large bowl; mash with a fork just until chunky. Stir in lime juice and remaining ingredients. Serve immediately.

CHILE CON QUESO

In most every Texas cook's pantry you will find a block of Velveeta. There is no substitute if you want smooth, creamy, addictive queso.

Makes *3 1/2 cups* · **Hands-on** *19 min.* · **Total** *44 min.*

1 1/4 lb. poblano peppers
1 jalapeño pepper
1/4 cup finely chopped onion
2 tsp. canola oil
1/4 tsp. ground cumin
1 garlic clove, minced
1 (16-oz.) package pasteurized prepared
   cheese product, cubed
1 (10-oz.) can diced tomatoes and green chiles
Tortilla chips

1. Preheat broiler.
2. Broil poblano and jalapeño pepper on a foil-lined baking sheet 5 inches from heat 4 to 5 minutes on each side or until peppers look blistered. Place peppers in a large zip-top plastic freezer bag; seal and let stand 10 minutes to loosen skins. Peel peppers; remove and discard seeds. Chop poblano peppers, and finely chop jalapeño pepper.
3. Meanwhile, sauté onion in hot oil in a medium-size saucepan over medium-high heat 5 minutes or until tender. Add cumin and garlic, and sauté 1 minute. Add cheese and tomatoes to saucepan. Reduce heat to medium, and cook, stirring constantly, 8 minutes or until cheese melts. Stir in peppers. Serve warm with tortilla chips.

SPICY GREEN CHILE QUESO

Green chiles are the hero of this queso and give the dip more of a West Texas vibe. Feel free to substitute sautéed fresh jalapeños or serranos for the green chiles if you'd like. This recipe is adapted from Austin's legendary Matt's Famous El Rancho restaurant.

Makes *3 cups* · **Hands-on** *25 min.* · **Total** *25 min.*

½ cup finely chopped onion
1 Tbsp. canola oil
2 garlic cloves, minced
½ tsp. kosher salt
½ tsp. ground cumin
½ (4-oz.) can diced jalapeños, undrained

1 (4-oz.) can chopped green chiles, drained
1 cup chopped tomato
8 oz. processed white American cheese, cubed
Corn or flour tortillas, tortilla chips

1. Sauté onion in hot oil in a medium-size nonstick saucepan over medium-high heat 3 minutes. Add garlic, and sauté 1 minute. Stir in salt, cumin, jalapeño peppers, and green chiles; sauté 1 minute.
2. Reduce heat to medium-low. Stir in tomato and cheese; cook, stirring often, 3 to 5 minutes or until cheese melts. Serve with tortillas or chips.

SALSA FIVE WAYS

As ketchup is to French fries and crackers are to cheese, salsa is to tortilla chips in Texas. A simple, blended mixture of tomato, onion, and jalapeño and you've got the classic base. From there, you can mix and match a variety of other ingredients to take the sauce in any number of directions from chunky or smooth, vinegary or smoky, tangy and tropical, and on into the sunset.

"NINFA'S" GREEN SAUCE,
page 151

AVOCADO MANGO SALSA,
page 150

SALSA FRESCA,
page 150

CRANBERRY SALSA,
page 152

**ROASTED TOMATO
AND ANCHO SALSA,**
page 153

TOMATILLO SALSA,
page 152

PICO de GALLO,
page 153

SALSA FRESCA *(pictured on page 148)*

A quick fresh salsa is key to livening up any Mexican-inspired dish. You can adjust ingredients any variety of ways, but this recipe is a good foundation for many spinoffs.

Makes *4 cups* · **Hands-on** *10 min.* · **Total** *10 min.*

6 cups coarsely chopped tomatoes
1 tsp. kosher salt
2 tsp. fresh lemon juice
1/2 cup firmly packed fresh cilantro leaves, coarsely chopped

1 jalapeño pepper, seeded and chopped
1 garlic clove, coarsely chopped
1/2 cup coarsely chopped red onion

Process all ingredients in a food processer, and pulse 8 to 10 times or to desired consistency. Cover and chill until ready to serve. Refrigerate in an airtight container up to 3 days.

TEXAS TOOLS

Molcajetes

A common tool in the Mexican and Mexican-American kitchen. The molcajete is essentially a mortar and pestle used to grind spices and salsas. Made of hand-carved lava rock, molcajetes are the most traditional, but need to be seasoned with dry rice ground into the bowl to smooth out any roughness. Continue to renew the dried rice until it no longer picks up color from the stone.

AVOCADO MANGO SALSA *(pictured on page 148)*

Mangoes are a heavenly treat, and while delicious on their own, their sweetness pairs so well with the creaminess of avocado and the tang of red onion and lime juice. Serve this as a topping for grilled fish, chicken, or pork, or serve it with tortilla chips and an assortment of other salsas for a little variety.

Makes *7 1/4 cups* · **Hands-on** *25 min.* · **Total** *25 min.*

5 cups diced ripe avocado (about 4 large)
1/3 cup fresh lime juice (about 3 limes)
3 cups diced ripe mango (about 3 medium)

1/4 cup diced red onion
1/4 cup chopped fresh cilantro
1 tsp. table salt

Combine avocado and lime juice in a bowl. Stir in mango and remaining ingredients. Refrigerate in an airtight container up to 3 days.

"NINFA'S" GREEN SAUCE *(pictured on page 148)*

Most everyone who has spent a lot of time in Houston knows the famed green sauce of The Original Ninfa's on Navigation. For years, it was a recipe well guarded by the restaurant until enough fanfare prodded them to graciously let the Houston Chronicle *print the sacred script. This is a variation of the original version with a little less sour cream, extra tomatillo, and a heaping squeeze of lime.*

Makes *6 1/2 cups* · **Hands-on** *25 min.* · **Total** *50 min.*

5 fresh tomatillos, husks removed
3 medium-size green tomatoes, chopped
2 jalapeño peppers, seeded and chopped
2 large garlic cloves, coarsely chopped
3 medium-size ripe avocados, halved

1/2 cup coarsely chopped fresh cilantro
2 tsp. table salt
1 cup sour cream
1 Tbsp. fresh lime juice
Tortilla chips

1. Chop tomatillos. Combine tomatillos and next 3 ingredients in a medium saucepan. Bring to a boil; cover, reduce heat to medium-low, and simmer 12 minutes. Remove from heat, and cool slightly.
2. Process tomatillo mixture, avocados, and next 2 ingredients in a blender or food processor until smooth, stopping to scrape down sides as needed. Transfer to a serving bowl. Stir in sour cream and lime juice. Serve warm or chilled with tortilla chips. Refrigerate in an airtight container up to 3 days.

CRANBERRY SALSA *(pictured on page 148)*

Move over, boring cranberry sauce. This zesty version of the favorite Thanksgiving condiment is wonderful any time of year. Try this with plaintain chips for a change of pace.

Makes *4 1/2 cups* · **Hands-on** *10 min.* · **Total** *10 min.*

1 Granny Smith apple, peeled and cut into
    8 wedges
1 cup coarsely chopped red onion
1 medium-size red bell pepper, coarsely
    chopped
1 jalapeño pepper, coarsely chopped
1 (12-oz.) package fresh or frozen
    cranberries, thawed
1/3 cup apple juice
1/4 cup sugar
1/4 cup chopped fresh cilantro
1 Tbsp. loosely packed lime zest
Plantain chips

1. Pulse first 5 ingredients in a food processor 4 to 6 times or until mixture is chunky, stopping to scrape sides as needed. Add apple juice and next 3 ingredients; pulse 3 times or to desired consistency.
2. Transfer salsa to a serving bowl. Stir in kosher salt to taste. Cover and chill until ready to serve. Serve with plantain chips. Refrigerate in an airtight container up to 2 days.

TOMATILLO SALSA *(pictured on page 149)*

Also called salsa verde, this goes well with chicken and pork.

Makes *4 cups* · **Hands-on** *10 min.* · **Total** *45 min.*

3 lb. fresh tomatillos, husks removed
2 jalapeño peppers, stemmed
1 Tbsp. fresh lime juice
4 garlic cloves
2 1/2 cups loosely packed cilantro
1 tsp. kosher salt

1. Combine tomatillos, peppers, and water to cover in a Dutch oven. Boil over medium-high heat; reduce heat, and simmer 10 minutes or until tomatillos are tender. Remove from heat; let stand 15 minutes. Drain. Wipe Dutch oven clean.
2. Process tomatillos, peppers, lime juice, and garlic in a blender to coarsely chop. Add cilantro; process until smooth. Return to Dutch oven and simmer over medium heat, stirring occasionally, 10 minutes until thickened slightly.
3. Remove from heat; stir in salt. Serve at room temperature, or cover and chill until ready to serve. Refrigerate in an airtight container up to 3 days.

ROASTED TOMATO AND ANCHO SALSA

(pictured on page 149)

Roasting vegetables adds a smoky depth to this salsa.

Makes *2 1/2 cups* · **Hands-on** *15 min.* · **Total** *2 hours, 50 min.*

1 dried ancho chile pepper
5 plum tomatoes, halved lengthwise
1 medium onion, quartered
1 large jalapeño pepper, halved and seeded

2 garlic cloves
3 Tbsp. fresh lime juice
1 tsp. kosher salt

1. Preheat oven to 450°F. Pour boiling water over ancho chile in a bowl or liquid measuring cup; let stand 20 minutes or until tender. Drain. Remove and discard stem and seeds.
2. Arrange tomatoes, onion, and jalapeño, cut sides down, in a single layer on a lightly greased aluminum foil-lined jelly-roll pan; sprinkle with garlic. Bake at 450°F for 30 minutes or until vegetables are tender; increase oven temperature to broil, and broil 5 minutes or until vegetables are blistered.
3. Pulse roasted vegetables in a food processor 6 to 8 times until mixture is chunky. Stop and scrape sides as necessary. Add ancho chile pepper to food processor; pulse to desired consistency. Stir in lime juice and salt. Chill in an airtight container up to 3 days.

PICO de GALLO *(pictured on page 149)*

This Mexican salsa is made from fresh ingredients. No cooking required!

Makes *3 1/2 cups* · **Hands-on** *10 min.* · **Total** *10 min.*

3 1/2 cups diced tomato
1 cup finely chopped red onion
1/4 cup loosely packed fresh cilantro, chopped

3 Tbsp. fresh lime juice
1/2 tsp. kosher salt
1 jalapeño pepper, minced

Stir together all ingredients in a bowl; toss gently to combine. Refrigerate in an airtight container up to 3 days.

MIGAS

Derived from the Spanish word for "crumbs," this breakfast dish is named for the leftover tortilla chip crumbs added to the scrambled egg mixture before removing from the stove-top to serve. The traditional Spanish and Portuguese version uses day-old bread and a few other ingredients, while this Tex-Mex version of Migas offers a different experience altogether. A side of warm flour tortillas and refried beans are common accompaniments.

Makes *8 servings* · **Hands-on** *15 min.* · **Total** *15 min.*

1 Tbsp. butter
3 green onions, chopped
1/4 cup finely chopped firm, ripe tomatoes
1 jalapeño pepper, seeded and finely
   chopped

12 large eggs, lightly beaten
1/2 tsp. kosher salt
1/2 tsp. freshly ground black pepper
3/4 cup crushed tortilla chips
1 cup shredded sharp Cheddar cheese

1. Melt butter in a large nonstick skillet over medium-high heat; add green onions, tomatoes, and jalapeño pepper, and sauté 2 minutes, stirring occasionally.
2. Whisk together eggs, salt, and pepper, and pour into skillet; cook, without stirring, 1 to 2 minutes or until eggs begin to set on bottom; fold in chips. Gently draw cooked edges away from sides and across bottom of skillet to form large curds, using a spatula. Repeat procedure, cooking until eggs are thickened but still moist (about 6 to 7 minutes). Fold in cheese during last minute of cooking. Serve immediately.

CHILAQUILES

The only thing complicated about Chilaquiles is its name. Pronounced "chill-ay-kee-us," this breakfast casserole is similar in flavor to tacos or nachos. The fried egg on top makes it even more delicious.

Makes *8 servings* · **Hands-on** *30 min.* · **Total** *50 min.*

1 onion, chopped
2 jalapeño peppers, seeded and chopped
2 garlic cloves, minced
¼ cup vegetable oil, divided
2 (14.5-oz.) cans diced tomatoes, undrained

5 oz. tortilla chips
3 cups shredded Mexican four-cheese blend
8 large eggs
Garnishes: avocado slices, chopped fresh cilantro

1. Preheat oven to 350°F. Sauté onion, jalapeño peppers, and garlic in 2 Tbsp. hot oil in a large nonstick skillet over medium-high heat 5 minutes or until tender. Stir in tomatoes; reduce heat to medium, and cook 10 minutes or until thickened.
2. Arrange tortilla chips in a greased 13- x 9-inch baking dish. Pour tomato mixture over chips, and sprinkle with cheese.
3. Bake at 350°F for 20 minutes or until cheese is bubbly.
4. Meanwhile, heat 1 Tbsp. oil in a large nonstick skillet over medium heat. Gently break 4 eggs into hot skillet. Cook 2 to 3 minutes on each side or to desired degree of doneness. Remove from skillet. Repeat procedure with remaining eggs and oil.
5. Cut casserole into 8 squares, and top each square with 1 fried egg. Serve warm with desired toppings.

MELISSA GUERRA

CHEF/COOKBOOK AUTHOR, MELISSA GUERRA
LATIN KITCHEN MARKET, SAN ANTONIO

Growing up on her family's cattle ranch near the Mexican border in South Texas, the food Melissa Guerra and her family ate was usually what was most readily available. It was not atypical to have a pot of beans and corn tortillas several days in a row.

With a landscape not unlike the uninhabitable Australian Outback, the South Texas terrain is a gnarly assortment of dry, cracked red earth and brambly limestone soil hospitable only to prickly cactus, wiry sage brush, and craggy mesquite trees. It's the type of setting Guerra was convinced turned the region's Native Americans into fierce, warring factions, raiding and pillaging for their own survival. Finding herself at a crossroads of two cultures, she wrote *Dishes from the Wild Horse Desert, Norteño Cooking of South Texas.*

"Food is more interesting because it follows the history about what kept people alive, not about what killed them," says Guerra. "It's something that can live on forever. Food has always been about more than just sustenance. It has a story to tell."

For Guerra, South Texas food is largely based on the lack of water to grow crops. "You don't see a lot of salad in the old cookbooks and kitchens from this area," says Guerra. "It took less water to raise a cow than to raise a crop, so that's what ended up on the plate. It was meat and beans that made it out here."

The way she views the evolution of South Texas cuisine is based on three "F's:" free, flourished, or favored. Free was anything found on the ground like tree berries, cactus, deer, and quail. Flourished were crops that grew well in the area like corn, beans, peaches, citrus, and sorghum. Favored refers to the specialty items like tea, coffee, and spices that people could get easily, especially after the railroads came in.

For Guerra, there was one crop that fulfilled all categories. "Chiles are all three."

Chile pequins are the native chile peppers to the Americas that propagated all of the major domestic chile varietals all over the world. They were free to the people of this area, but as a commodity they also flourished in about every culture they were eventually traded to. The Spanish traded chiles as a spicy flavor alternative to black pepper, which was much more expensive. As a cooking ingredient, they were particularly favored for their flavor as well as their medicinal properties.

When it comes to modern day Tex-Mex, the one distinct flavor that sets South Texas Tex-Mex apart from the rest of Texas is mesquite.

"That's the only thing people could use to cook with out here," says Guerra. "It adds this sweetness to the food that you don't get from other Tex-Mex. In other parts of the state they use post oak or pecan, but that's what grows for them. South Texas Tex-Mex has a unique mesquite flavor to it. It's what I miss the most when I travel away from home for a while."

> *"Food has always been about more than just sustenance. It has a story to tell."*

Masa Dough

1/4 lb. pork lard (about 1/2 cup)

2 1/2 lb. freshly ground masa

2 tsp. sea salt

1 1/3 cups reserved warm pork broth from Meat Filling (page 160)

1. Beat lard at medium speed with an electric mixer 2 minutes.
2. Stir together masa and next 2 ingredients in a bowl until well blended. Gradually add masa mixture to lard, beating at medium speed just until blended after each addition. Cover until ready to use.

Note: If you can't find fresh masa, whisk together 3 cups masa harina (corn flour) 1 1/2 Tbsp. all-purpose flour, 1 1/2 tsp. baking powder, and 1 1/2 tsp. salt. Whisk in 2 1/4 cups very hot water until dry ingredients are moistened. (Add more hot water 1 tsp. at a time.) Knead 3 to 4 times to make a smooth dough.

Makes *about 4 lb.*
Hands-on *15 min.*
Total *15 min.*

MELISSA GUERRA'S TAMALES

Fresh corn tamales are a Latin holiday favorite. These are fantastic on their own or top with salsa, pepper slices, or crumbled cheese.

Makes *3 dozen* · **Hands-on** *2 hours* · **Total** *4 hours, 30 min.*

1 (8-oz.) package dried cornhusks

MEAT FILLING
1 (4¹/₂-lb.) bone-in pork shoulder roast
   (Boston butt), meat cubed
5 garlic cloves, 2 crushed and 3 minced
1 onion, quartered
2 bay leaves

4¹/₂ tsp. table salt, divided
13 dried ancho chile peppers (about 4 oz.)
2 oz. pork lard (about ¹/₄ cup)
¹/₂ tsp. freshly ground black pepper
¹/₂ tsp. ground cumin

Masa Dough (page 159)
2¹/₄ cups Meat Filling

1. Soak husks in hot water 1 to 1¹/₂ hours or until softened.
2. While husks soak, prepare Meat Filling: Bring pork, bone, crushed garlic, onion, bay leaves, 2 tsp. salt, and water to cover to a boil in an 8-qt. stockpot. Cover, reduce heat, and simmer 1 hour or until meat is done.
3. Pour through a wire-mesh strainer into a bowl, discarding bay leaves, onion, and garlic. Remove any bits of pork from bone; discard bone. Reserve broth. Pulse half of cooked pork in a food processor until finely chopped. Reserve remaining pork for another use.
4. Pour boiling water to cover ancho chiles in a bowl; let stand 20 minutes. Drain. Remove and discard stems and seeds. Process peppers, 1¹/₃ cups reserved pork broth, and 2 minced garlic cloves in a blender or food processor until smooth, adding additional broth if necessary. Pour mixture through a wire-mesh strainer into a bowl; discard solids. Reserve 1¹/₃ cups broth for Masa Dough and remaining broth for another use.
5. Melt lard in a large Dutch oven over medium-high heat. Add freshly ground black pepper, cumin, and remaining 2¹/₂ tsp. salt and 1 minced garlic clove. Sauté 10 seconds. Add ancho chile mixture, and sauté 2 minutes. Stir in minced pork. Season with salt and pepper to taste. Simmer, stirring occasionally, 10 minutes or until most of liquid evaporates. Remove from heat, and cool completely (about 30 minutes).
6. Prepare Tamales: Drain husks, and pat dry.
7. Spread about ¹/₄ cup Masa Dough onto 1 side of each husk, leaving a 3-inch border at bottom narrow edge and a 1-inch border at straight sides.
8. Spoon 1 heaping tablespoonful Meat Filling over Masa Dough. Fold sides of husk over, enclosing filling completely. Fold bottom end with 3-inch border over folded sides. Repeat procedure using remaining Masa Dough and Meat Filling. Freeze remaining meat filling for making a second batch of tamales another time.
9. Arrange half the tamales in a steamer basket set over a stockpot; add water to fill just below basket. Bring to a boil, cover, and steam 45 minutes or until filling is set. Add boiling water as needed. Remove to a serving platter; keep warm. Repeat procedure.

Note: Tamales may be tied with strips of corn husk to secure, if desired.

TEXAS TOOLS

16-qt. Enamel Steamer for Tamales

Enameled cookware is the choice in many homes when it comes to cooking for a large batch of tamales. Choose a three-piece steamer set that includes a stockpot, a steamer insert, and lid. The size is not too big for those beginner batches of tamales.

GRAPEFRUIT, AVOCADO, AND BUTTER LETTUCE SALAD

In the winter, the Rio Grande Valley is alive with orchards of juicy red grapefruit. Tender butter lettuce paired with creamy avocado slices, toasted pine nuts, and the brightness of grapefruit is a fantastic combination everyone is sure to love.

Makes *6 to 8 servings* · **Hands-on** *20 min.* · **Total** *20 min.*

2 large red grapefruit
2 heads butter lettuce, torn
2 ripe avocados, sliced

⅓ cup toasted pine nuts
Citrus Vinaigrette (recipe follows)
Garnish: fresh cilantro leaves

1. Using a sharp, thin-bladed knife, cut a ¼-inch-thick slice from each end of each grapefruit. Place flat-end down on a cutting board, and remove peel in strips, cutting from top to bottom following the curvature of fruit. Remove any bitter white pith. Holding peeled grapefruit in the palm of your hand, slice between membranes, and gently remove whole segments.
2. Divide lettuce among 6 to 8 serving plates. Top each serving with grapefruit segments and avocado slices; sprinkle with pine nuts. Drizzle with desired amount of Citrus Vinaigrette, and add salt and pepper to taste.

CITRUS VINAIGRETTE

Makes *⅔ cup* · **Hands-on** *5 min.* · **Total** *5 min.*

¼ cup fresh orange juice
2 Tbsp. fresh lime juice
½ tsp. sugar

½ tsp. table salt
¼ tsp. freshly ground black pepper
¼ cup olive oil

Whisk together first 5 ingredients in a small bowl. Add oil in a slow, steady stream, whisking until smooth. Refrigerate in an airtight container up to 5 days.

TEXAS TIDBIT

TEXAS CITRUS: RED GRAPEFRUIT

A hybrid between a pummelo and the sweet orange, the grapefruit was most likely brought to Texas by Spanish or French explorers by way of Florida. The first reported grapefruit grove was in the Lower Rio Grande Valley of South Texas in the late 1800s. The subtropical climate, fertile soil, and sunny weather here turned out to be ideal. The unexpected discovery of a red grapefruit in 1929 gave rise to the Texas Red grapefruit industry and an eventual patent. Dr. Richard Hensz of the A&M Citrus Center developed a deeper red grapefruit he named the Star Ruby variety in 1970 and the Rio Red variety in 1984. Today, Texas markets two trademarked fruits: Ruby-Sweet and Rio Star.

SMOKED CHICKEN TORTILLA SOUP

Everyone in Texas has a particular version of tortilla soup. This rendition uses smoked chicken to add extra depth of flavor. New Mexico chile powder is a single-chile powder made from grinding dried New Mexico chiles and should not be confused with chili powder, which is a seasoning blend. To speed up things, feel free to use two rotisserie chickens from the deli section of your local grocery store.

Makes *8 to 10 servings* · **Hands-on** *25 min.* · **Total** *1 hour, 20 min.*

1 large onion, diced
1 large jalapeño pepper, seeded and
   chopped
3 Tbsp. olive oil
3 garlic cloves, chopped
8 cups chicken broth
1 (15.25-oz.) can whole kernel corn,
   drained*
1 (15-oz.) can black beans, drained
1 (14.5-oz.) can fire-roasted diced
   tomatoes

1 (14.5-oz.) can diced tomatoes with chiles
3 Tbsp. ground cumin
1 1/2 Tbsp. New Mexico chile powder
1 1/2 tsp. table salt
1 tsp. Worcestershire sauce
5 cups coarsely chopped Smoked Chicken
   (page 223)
Toppings: tortilla strips, fresh cilantro,
   avocado slices, lime slices, crumbled
   queso fresco

1. Sauté onion and jalapeño pepper in hot oil in a Dutch oven over medium-high heat 5 to 6 minutes. Add garlic, and sauté 1 to 2 minutes.
2. Stir in broth and next 8 ingredients. Bring to a boil; reduce heat, and simmer 40 minutes.
3. Remove from heat, and stir in chicken. Let stand 10 minutes before serving. Serve with desired toppings.

*3 to 4 ears fresh corn may be substituted for canned corn. Remove husks, and cut kernels from cobs.

PORK CARNITAS

The great thing about making carnitas is that you there's not a whole lot of hands-on work that you have to do to make a really great meal. Of course, waiting five hours for the slow-cooking process is something to keep in mind. A lot of people serve the pork after it's been shredded, but I like to take it a step further by crisping up the shredded meat in a frying pan. Serve with a dollop of "Ninfa's" Green Sauce (page 151).

Makes *8 servings* · **Hands-on** *40 min.* · **Total** *5 hours, 45 min.*

1 (4-lb.) boneless pork shoulder roast (Boston butt), trimmed and cut into 2- to 3-inch pieces
1 (12-oz.) bottle Mexican beer
1 large onion, quartered
1 cup fresh orange juice
1/2 cup fresh lime juice
5 garlic cloves, halved
1 Tbsp. table salt
2 tsp. freshly ground black pepper

2 tsp. chili powder
1 tsp. dried oregano
1 tsp. ground cumin
2 Tbsp. olive oil
24 corn tortillas, warmed
1 1/2 cups crumbled queso fresco (fresh Mexican cheese)
1/2 cup chopped fresh cilantro
2 limes, cut into wedges

1. Combine first 11 ingredients in a 5-qt. round slow cooker. Cover and cook on LOW 5 hours or until meat is fork-tender.
2. Remove pork from slow cooker; shred with 2 forks.
3. Cook pork, in batches, in hot oil in a large skillet over medium-high heat, stirring often, 3 minutes or until edges of pork begin to brown.
4. Serve pork in warm tortillas with cheese, cilantro, and lime wedges.

TEXAS PIT STOPS

CHRIS MADRID'S
San Antonio

DELIA'S TAMALES
McAllen

MI TIERRA RESTAURANT & BAKERY
San Antonio

LA FONDA ON MAIN
San Antonio

POLLOS ASADOS LOS NORTEÑOS
San Antonio

VERA'S BACKYARD BAR-B-QUE
Brownsville

KING RANCH CHICKEN

Hailing from an era when casseroles were king, this Tex-Mex addition reigns supreme as the staple dish for church suppers and neighborhood potlucks. Though not an invention of the famed King Ranch—it's more likely the invention of a lady's Junior League—the spicy flavors of chili powder, roasted peppers, and cumin never fail to please.

Makes *12 servings* · **Hands-on** *1 hour* · **Total** *1 hour, 40 min.*

Vegetable cooking spray
6 Tbsp. butter
1 1/2 cups chopped onion
1 cup chopped red bell pepper
1 cup chopped poblano peppers (about 2 medium peppers)
1 jalapeño pepper, seeded and chopped
2 garlic cloves, chopped
1 Tbsp. chili powder
1 Tbsp. ground cumin
1 tsp. kosher salt
1/2 tsp. freshly ground black pepper
1/4 cup all-purpose flour

1 3/4 cups chicken broth
1 (10-oz.) can diced tomatoes with green chiles, drained
1 1/2 cups sour cream
2 lb. Smoked Chicken (page 223), coarsely chopped (about 5 cups)
1 cup loosely packed fresh cilantro leaves, chopped
2 cups shredded Monterey Jack cheese
2 cups shredded sharp Cheddar cheese
18 (6-inch) corn tortillas
1/4 cup canola oil
Garnish: chopped fresh cilantro

1. Preheat oven to 375°F. Lightly grease a 13- x 9-inch baking dish with cooking spray.
2. Melt butter in a large skillet over medium-high heat. Add onion and next 3 ingredients; sauté 8 to 10 minutes or until tender and lightly browned. Add garlic, chili powder, cumin, salt, and pepper, and cook 1 minute.
3. Sprinkle flour over vegetable mixture, and cook, stirring constantly, 1 minute. Whisk in broth, and bring to a boil, stirring constantly. Boil 1 to 2 minutes or until thickened. Remove from heat. Add tomatoes and sour cream.
4. Stir together chicken and cilantro; stir in vegetable mixture until blended.
5. Combine cheeses in a small bowl.
6. Heat a large cast-iron skillet over high heat. Lightly brush each tortilla on both sides with oil. Cook tortillas, in batches, in hot skillet until lightly browned and crisp on both sides.
7. Line bottom of prepared baking dish with 6 tortillas, overlapping slightly, to cover bottom of dish. Top with half of chicken mixture and one-third of cheese. Repeat layers once. Top with remaining tortillas and cheese. Lightly coat a sheet of aluminum foil with cooking spray, and cover baking dish.
8. Bake at 375°F for 20 minutes. Uncover and bake 10 more minutes or until bubbly and lightly browned on top. Let stand 10 minutes before serving.

CHICKEN FAJITAS

In the 1980s, chicken fajitas began to show up on Tex-Mex menus as an alternative to beef. Perhaps it appeared as a way to offer a healthier option for diners, but whatever the reason, most people who make them at home tend to take as much pride in their chicken fajita recipe as they do for the original beef version.

Makes *6 to 8 servings* · **Hands-on** *20 min.* · **Total** *2 hours, 30 min.*

$\frac{1}{2}$ cup white wine Worcestershire sauce
$\frac{1}{2}$ cup dry white wine
$\frac{1}{2}$ cup soy sauce
5 skinned and boned chicken breasts
$\frac{1}{4}$ cup Texas Meat Rub (page 13)

12 to 16 (6-inch) fajita-size flour tortillas, warmed
Toppings: Pico de Gallo (page 153), Simple Guacamole (page 146), shredded Cheddar cheese, sour cream

1. Stir together first 3 ingredients. Pour marinade into a large shallow dish or zip-top plastic freezer bag; add chicken. Cover or seal, and chill 2 hours, turning once.
2. Preheat grill to 350° to 400°F (medium-high) heat. Remove chicken from marinade, discarding marinade. Rub chicken with Texas Meat Rub. Grill chicken, covered with grill lid, 5 to 6 minutes on each side or until done. Remove chicken from grill, and let stand 10 minutes. Cut chicken diagonally across the grain into thin strips. Serve chicken in warm tortillas with desired toppings.

TEXAS TOOLS

Tortilla Press

If making tortillas from scratch, you could do it the old-fashioned way and pat the tortillas back and forth between your hands. But the most efficient way is with a tortilla press. You can use plastic wrap or wax paper placed on either side of the dough and then use the handheld press to yield a perfectly round and flat tortilla for cooking.

ENCHILADAS SUIZAS

Enchiladas Suizas are often smothered with a creamy white sauce, but here, Mexican crema enriches Tomatillo Salsa. Serve this comfort food favorite with Baked Mexican Rice (page 192) or Black Beans (page 193).

Makes *8 to 10 servings* · **Hands-on** *30 min.* · **Total** *1 hour, 25 min.*

Tomatillo Salsa (page 152)
1 (15-oz.) container crema, divided*
½ tsp. kosher salt
4 cups shredded Smoked Chicken
    (page 223)**
2 cups shredded Chihuahua or Muenster
    cheese, divided

1 (8-oz.) package shredded Mexican four-
    cheese blend, divided
20 (6-inch) corn tortillas
⅓ cup vegetable oil
1 cup finely chopped onion
⅓ cup chopped fresh cilantro
Additional crema (optional)

1. Preheat oven to 375°F. Heat Tomatillo Salsa in a 3-qt. saucepan over medium heat, stirring occasionally, 6 minutes or until hot. Stir in 1¼ cups crema and salt. Reduce heat to low; keep warm, stirring occasionally.
2. Combine chicken, remaining crema, 1 cup Chihuahua cheese, and ½ cup Mexican four-cheese blend.
3. Heat a large nonstick skillet over medium heat. Brush oil on each side of tortillas. Cook tortillas, in batches, in hot skillet 10 to 20 seconds on each side until softened. Pat with paper towels to remove excess oil. Cover with aluminum foil to keep warm.
4. Spoon about ¼ cup chicken mixture on edge of 1 tortilla, and roll up tortilla. Place in a lightly greased 13- x 9-inch baking dish, seam sides down. Repeat with remaining tortillas and chicken mixture. Pour salsa mixture over enchiladas, gently shaking dish to coat evenly. Sprinkle with remaining 1 cup Chihuahua cheese and remaining 1½ cups Mexican cheese.
5. Bake at 375°F for 45 minutes or until golden brown and bubbly. Remove from oven; let stand 10 minutes before serving. Top each serving with onion, cilantro, and additional crema, if desired.

*Heavy cream or crème fraîche may be substituted for crema.
**Store-bought smoked or rotisserie chicken may be substituted for Smoked Chicken.

TEX-MEX CUISINE

Tex-Mex cuisine is defined by history, flavor, and evolution. Without question, it's influenced heavily by Mexico. More specifically by the northern states of the country that border Texas including Chihuahua, Coahuila, Nuevo Leon, and Tamaulipas. But rather than simply taking ownership of another culture's cuisine, Texas managed to put its stamp on things weaving pieces of Texas ranching, German immigration, and the early coastal fishing industries into the fabric of a new Tex-Mex cuisine.

Texas' history includes many times where the state's current boundaries were part of Mexico. Much of South Texas was once known as the Nueces Strip, stemming from the time when Texas claimed the Rio Grande as its southern border while Mexico claimed the Nueces River, 150 miles north of the Rio Grande. Both countries fought over the land until 1848 when Mexico ceded the Nueces Strip to the U.S. in the Treaty of Guadalupe Hidalgo. Not surprisingly, South Texas cuisine is largely influenced by Mexican flavors. Early staples included corn, beans, meat, chiles, spices and cactus pads (napoles), and cactus flowers (tunas).

Along the western stretches of the state is a deep-rooted connection to New Mexico, which is known for a fusion of Native American and Spanish-Mexican flavors. Historically, New Mexico—and even parts of Colorado, Kansas, Oklahoma, and Wyoming—was once a part of Texas. In fact, when Texas first entered the United States in the 1840s, the geographical boundary lines curved north to stretch through a part of New Mexico that included Santa Fe.

As a result, West Texas cuisine is heavily influenced by the green chile. Referred to by a number of synonyms including Anaheim chile, New Mexico chile, long green chile, Hatch chile, and sometimes Chimayo chile—all of which are slightly different from one another— the distinctive green chile is the primary chile ingredient for sauces, soups, and chile powders in this portion of the state.

Anglo-American cattle ranchers from Europe and parts of the Southern United States brought along traditional and Southern-style cooking as well as the addition of flour to standard pantry items. Before long, a blend of flavors transpired into the early beginnings of Tex-Mex food.

Originally dismissed by iconic Mexican chef and writer, Diana Kennedy in the 1970s, it wasn't until the late 20th century that Tex-Mex in its most basic form was given credibility by the many Texans who had come to embrace it as their own.

Award-winning food writer and historian Robb Walsh released *The Tex-Mex Cookbook* in 2004 uncovering a century timeline of Tex-Mex food from the early introduction of chili at the Chicago World's Fair by a San Antonio chili stand in 1893, to a time through the late 1980s and '90s when restaurants across the state were proudly displaying the term on their street signs and menus.

Walsh thanked Kennedy in his book for "convincing us that Tex-Mex wasn't really Mexican food, she forced us to realize that it was something far more interesting: America's oldest regional cuisine."

TEX-MEX

There's an underlying joke that the various dishes on a Tex-Mex menu are essentially the same ingredients rearranged into a different formation and given a different name. You be the judge. Among the most beloved dishes in Tex-Mex fare are fajitas, enchiladas, tacos, and nachos with the occasional burrito thrown in. Assorted side dishes include: refried beans, Mexican rice, guacamole, salsa fresca, and plenty of chile con queso.

CHEESE ENCHILADAS CON CARNE

Cheese enchiladas are smothered with Enchilada Gravy in Texas, but for a heartier Tex-Mex spin, try this beefed-up version.

Makes *12 servings* · **Hands-on** *45 min.* · **Total** *2 hours, including gravy*

10 dried ancho chile peppers
5 dried chipotle chile peppers
3 cups beef broth, divided
1 1/4 tsp. kosher salt, divided
1 tsp. ground cumin
1/2 tsp. dried Mexican oregano

3 1/4 cups chopped white onion
1/2 cup plus 2 Tbsp. vegetable oil, divided
3 garlic cloves, chopped
1 to 1 1/2 lb. ground beef
24 (6-inch) yellow corn tortillas
8 cups shredded Mexican-blend cheese

1. Preheat oven to 375°F. Pour boiling water over dried chiles in a bowl; let sit 15 minutes or until tender; drain. Remove and discard stems and seeds. Process peppers, 1 cup broth, 1 tsp. salt, cumin, and oregano in a food processor until smooth.
2. Sauté onion and remaining salt in 2 Tbsp. hot oil in a stockpot over medium heat 6 minutes. Add garlic; sauté 2 minutes. Add beef; cook 8 minutes or until no longer pink.
3. Stir pepper mixture into beef mixture, and cook 3 minutes. Stir in remaining 2 cups broth. Bring to a boil; reduce heat and simmer, stirring occasionally, 30 minutes.
4. Brush remaining oil on each side of tortillas. Cook, in batches, in hot skillet 10 to 20 seconds on each side until softened. Remove excess oil with paper towels. Keep warm.
5. Spoon 1/4 cup cheese on edge of 1 tortilla, and roll up. Place in a greased 13- x 9-inch baking dish, seam sides down. Repeat, filling a second baking dish. Pour beef mixture over top. Sprinkle each with remaining 2 cups cheese. Bake, covered, 10 minutes; uncover and bake 10 more minutes or until cheese is melted. Let stand 5 minutes.

ENCHILADA GRAVY

Makes *2 1/2 cups* · **Hands-on** *25 min.* · **Total** *35 min.*

3/4 cup coarsely chopped onion
2 garlic cloves
6 Tbsp. vegetable oil
1/4 cup all-purpose flour
2 Tbsp. chili powder

1 tsp. table salt
2 tsp. ground cumin
1 tsp. freshly ground black pepper
1/2 tsp. dried Mexican oregano
2 1/2 cups beef broth

1. Process onion and garlic in a blender 30 seconds or until smooth.
2. Heat oil in a saucepan over medium heat. Whisk in flour; cook 3 minutes until golden. Whisk in onion mixture; cook 1 minute. Reduce heat to medium-low. Add chili powder and next 4 ingredients. Reduce heat to low. Add broth, whisking 5 minutes or until thickened. Remove from heat; let stand 10 minutes. Pour over cheese enchiladas before baking.

SAN ANTONIO PUFFY TACOS

Original tacos were a little different than the stale, fried corn tortillas machine-pressed into a U-shaped envelope— an invention of fast food chain entrepreneur Glen Bell of the famed Taco Bell. The real deal begins with a ball of masa flattened into a thin round that is fried to a golden crispness. The masa puffs up a bit, which is how the moniker "puffy taco" came into play. Stuff with ground taco meat, shredded lettuce, diced tomatoes, and shredded cheese.

Makes *8 to 9 servings* · **Hands-on** *1 hour, 5 min.* · **Total** *1 hour, 20 min.*

2 lb. fresh Masa Dough (page 159)
Wax paper
Vegetable oil
1 onion, chopped
1 jalapeño pepper, seeded and minced
2 garlic cloves, minced
1 lb. ground beef
2 plum tomatoes, chopped

4 tsp. chili powder
1 Tbsp. ground cumin
1 tsp. table salt
$^1/_2$ cup Mexican beer
Toppings: shredded cheese, shredded iceberg lettuce, sour cream, fresh salsa, guacamole

1. Shape masa dough into 18 golf-ball-sized (about 2 Tbsp.) portions. Cut sides off a zip-top plastic freezer bag. Line top and bottom of a tortilla press with freezer bag. Place masa rounds in freezer bag within tortilla press, and close, forming round tortillas. (If you don't have a tortilla press, use a flat plate, skillet, or flat-bottomed bowl, and press masa balls into flat rounds against countertop between sheets of wax paper. To ensure even thickness, press dough rounds once, rotate 180°, and press again.) Gently stack uncooked masa rounds between layers of wax paper.
2. Pour oil to depth of 3 inches into a Dutch oven; heat to 375°F.
3. Gently lower 1 uncooked tortilla into hot oil. Once tortilla rises to surface and begins to bubble, cook 10 seconds. Gently flip tortilla, and lightly press center of tortilla, using a metal spatula, to create a U-shape. Cook 30 seconds or until golden brown. Carefully remove from oil, sprinkle with salt and drain upside down on a paper towel-lined wire rack. Repeat procedure with remaining tortillas. Keep tortillas warm until ready to serve.
4. Cook onion and next 2 ingredients in 2 Tbsp. hot oil in a large nonstick skillet over medium-high heat 4 to 5 minutes or until softened. Add beef, and cook, stirring often, 8 minutes or until meat crumbles and is no longer pink; drain.
5. Return beef mixture to skillet; add tomatoes, chili powder, cumin, and salt, and cook over medium heat 4 minutes. Add beer and reduce heat to medium-low. Cover and simmer 15 minutes. Uncover, and cook 3 minutes or until liquid is absorbed.
6. Serve beef in warm tortillas with desired toppings.

TEXAS TIDBIT

CORN TORTILLAS

When it comes to ingredients most easily cultivated in Mexico, and by extension, South Texas, corn was among one of the most used commodities. The most common use for corn was in the form of tortillas. Spanish for "little cakes," tortillas were made from corn that was ground together with water or lyme on a metate, a three-legged stone table. What was left was a dense dough called masa. As you'll find in the recipe for puffy tacos (at right), the masa was rolled into a ball, pressed into a flat round using a tortilla press, and either heated on a flat cast-iron comal, or griddle, or fried until crispy.

AMIGO PIE

Known to some as Tamale Pie, this one-dish meal is great for busy weeknights because it's quick, easy, and filling. Our family changed the name because it bears no resemblance to a tamale, but whatever you call it, it's sure to draw everyone to the table.

Makes *8 servings* · **Hands-on** *20 min.* · **Total** *53 min.*

1 cup chopped onion
1 lb. ground chuck
1 cup sliced black olives, divided
1 Tbsp. chili powder
1 tsp. table salt, divided
$^{1}/_{2}$ tsp. freshly ground black pepper
1 medium tomato, diced
$^{3}/_{4}$ cup plain yellow cornmeal

$^{1}/_{4}$ cup all-purpose flour
$^{1}/_{2}$ tsp. baking powder
1 cup hot water
2 Tbsp. butter, melted
1 $^{1}/_{2}$ cups (6 oz.) shredded sharp Cheddar cheese, divided
Garnish: sour cream and fresh cilantro leaves

1. Preheat oven to 400°F.
2. Cook onion and beef in a large skillet over medium-high heat, stirring often, 6 to 8 minutes or until meat crumbles and is no longer pink; drain. Wipe skillet clean. Return beef mixture to skillet. Add $^{1}/_{2}$ cup olives, chili powder, $^{1}/_{2}$ tsp. salt, pepper, and tomato. Cook 2 to 3 minutes or until onion is tender. Remove from heat.
3. Stir together cornmeal, flour, baking powder, and remaining $^{1}/_{2}$ tsp. salt. Whisk in 1 cup hot water and melted butter, stirring until batter is smooth. Stir in 1 cup cheese and remaining $^{1}/_{2}$ cup olives.
4. Pour batter into a lightly greased 9-inch pie plate. Spread beef filling over batter, leaving a $^{1}/_{2}$-inch border around the outside edges. Sprinkle evenly with remaining $^{1}/_{2}$ cup cheese.
5. Bake at 400°F for 23 to 28 minutes or until crust is golden brown and set. Let stand 10 minutes before serving.

TEXAS TIDBIT

TEXAS ONIONS

Texas grows more sweet onions than any other vegetable crop. In 1898, settlers sprinkled Bermuda onion seeds near the South Texas town of Cotulla, and by 1904 there were more than 500 acres of the Caribbean transplant in South Texas. By 1920, Texas was out-producing the Bermuda islands. The primary onions produced and exported over the better part of the following century were from Texas, including the hybrid Granax, which was planted in many other states under different names including the well-known Georgia Vidalia onion.

In the 1980s, Leonard Pike and Paul Leeper of Texas A&M found hybrid 1015Y to be one of the best onions to mature early and offer a sweet, mild taste. This Texas onion is so sweet some say you can eat it like an apple.

BEEF FAJITAS

What once was a way to use up lowly scraps of meat and pay Mexican vacqueros for working a day on the cattle ranches of South and West Texas, beef fajitas are now one of the most-loved Tex-Mex dishes. The secret to this version is the marinade that gives the beef its wonderful flavor and texture. Serve with grilled red onion and jalapeños and wedges of lime.

Makes *6 to 8 servings* · **Hands-on** *24 min.* · **Total** *3 hours, 24 min.*

7 Tbsp. Texas Meat Rub (page 13), divided
3/4 cup beer
1/2 cup fresh lime juice (about 3 to 4 medium limes)
1/2 cup Worcestershire sauce
1/3 cup amber agave nectar
1/4 cup soy sauce
1 (3-lb.) flank steak

12 to 16 (6-inch) fajita-size flour tortillas, warmed
Toppings: Pico de Gallo (page 153), Simple Guacamole (page 146), shredded Cheddar cheese, sour cream, sliced red onions, sliced jalapeños

1. Whisk together 1/4 cup Texas Meat Rub and next 5 ingredients in medium saucepan. Bring to a light boil over medium heat; reduce heat to medium-low, and simmer, whisking constantly, 5 minutes. Remove from heat, and let cool 5 minutes.
2. Place steak in a large baking dish; pour warm marinade over steak. Cover and chill at least 3 hours.
3. Preheat grill to 350° to 400°F (medium-high) heat. Remove steak from marinade, discarding marinade. Rub both sides of steak with remaining 3 Tbsp. Texas Meat Rub.
4. Grill steak, covered with grill lid, 3 to 5 minutes on each side or to desired degree of doneness. Remove from grill, and let stand 10 minutes. Cut steak diagonally across the grain into thin strips. Serve steak in warm tortillas with desired toppings.

TEXAS TOOLS

Tortilla Warmer

This may seem like a frivolous item, but if you want your tortillas (corn or flour) to be warm, pliable, and void of gumminess or dryness, use a comal (see page 144). Stack the warm tortillas in a tortilla warmer and they'll remain perfect every time. Tortilla warmers run the gamut. They range from elaborately painted clay to hand-woven grass, and thick plastic.

JOHNNY HERNANDEZ

CHEF/RESTAURATEUR, LA GLORIA, EL MACHITO, LA FRUTERIA, TRUE FLAVORS, SAN ANTONIO

Restaurant life is a family tradition for Johnny Hernandez. He grew up in San Antonio, and his father was a first generation Mexican-American who worked at the iconic Earl Abel's diner for a number of years learning the ins and outs of American comfort food before opening up his own Mexican restaurant on the west side of town. That's where Johnny and his brother and sister cut their teeth in the business.

As kids, they would play out back behind his dad's restaurant with aromas of fresh-baked treats from the next door Mexican panaderia (bakery) mingling with the smell of freshly made tortillas from the nearby molino (a corn mill for tortillas and tortilla chips). The foods Hernandez enjoyed on a daily basis included everything from barbacoa and carnitas to tamales and beans with fresh homemade tortillas.

Hernandez and his siblings eventually found themselves working at the restaurant. He enjoyed the kitchen so much that he dedicated himself to attending the Culinary Institute of America in New York right after high school. Hernandez worked in luxury hotel restaurants in Las Vegas and Santa Barbara but couldn't shake his longing for the simple foods from home. In 1994, he returned to San Antonio and opened a catering business called True Flavors. He also took time for a few excursions to the interior of Mexico to discover more of the flavors of his heritage.

"My mom is really the one who lured me down there," says Hernandez. "She is a missionary and had me join her each summer to cook for a kids' camp in Central Mexico near Guanajuato."

His primary experience with the cuisine was from Monterrey, along the Texas border, where the most common range of Mexican food he encountered was tacos, carne asada, flautas, and quesadillas. After volunteering for the camp for more than ten seasons, he couldn't help but let the rich flavors of the different Mexican regions inspire him.

"I was fascinated by the ingredients and methods used for these delicious dishes. They were so similar to what I'd grown up around, but there was also this celebration about it," says Hernandez.

In 2010 Hernandez opened La Gloria at The Pearl drawing on familiar Tex-Mex items like tacos, ceviche, and quesadillas but also reflecting the culinary wealth he discovered in the pueblitos, mountains, and coastal villages of Mexico. Items like Michoacán-style carnitas, tortas ahogadas of Guadalajara, Oaxacan tlayudas, and rich mole xiqueño from Veracruz could be found on the menu.

He's also launched a fruit stand and tapas bar called the Fruteria, a mesquite grill kitchen called El Machito preparing traditional carne asadas of northern Mexico and estilo-campestre of Guadalajara as a tribute to the parrilleros (grill chefs) of the country, and a special event space, Casa Hernán, that hosts elaborate weddings and private parties catered with Mexican-inspired cuisine.

"I was fascinated by the ingredients and methods used for these delicious dishes."

ARRACHERA EN ADOBO

A favorite traditional dish from Chef Johnny Hernandez, serve this traditional taco filling with sour cream, avocado, tomatillo salsa, and warm tortillas. It will become a favorite.

Makes *6 servings* · **Hands-on** *50 min.* · **Total** *3 hours, 25 min., including adobo*

4 lb. flank or skirt steak
¹/₂ tsp. table salt
¹/₄ cup vegetable oil
1 onion, diced
10 garlic cloves, minced

Ancho and Pasilla Adobo (recipe follows)
1¹/₂ tsp. whole cumin seeds, toasted and ground
2 cups tomato puree

1. Sprinkle steak with salt. Brown, in batches, 3 to 4 minutes on each side in hot oil in a large Dutch oven over medium-high heat. Remove; reserve drippings in Dutch oven.
2. Sauté onion and garlic in hot drippings 5 minutes. Add Ancho and Pasilla Adobo, cumin, tomato puree, steak, and any accumulated juices from steak to Dutch oven.
3. Bring to a light boil. Add 2 cups water, and season with salt to taste. Cover, reduce heat to low, and simmer 2 hours or until meat is tender. Remove steak from Dutch oven, and let stand 15 minutes. Cut steak diagonally across the grain into thin slices.
4. Meanwhile, cook sauce, uncovered, 15 minutes or until thickened. Serve with steak.

ANCHO AND PASILLA ADOBO

Makes *3¹/₂ cups* · **Hands-on** *20 min.* · **Total** *30 min.*

8 dried ancho chile peppers
10 dried pasilla peppers
1¹/₂ tsp. whole cumin seeds
1¹/₂ tsp. dried Mexican oregano

1 cup fresh orange juice
¹/₂ cup fresh lime juice
¹/₃ cup firmly packed brown sugar
2 Tbsp. pureed Roasted Garlic (at left)

1. Preheat oven to 350°F. Place ancho chile and pasilla peppers on a baking sheet. Bake at 350°F for 5 minutes. Remove from oven. Pour boiling water to cover peppers in a bowl; let stand 5 minutes or until tender. Drain, reserving water. Discard stems and seeds.
2. Place a small skillet over medium-high heat until hot; add cumin seeds and oregano, and cook, stirring constantly, 1 minute or until toasted. Remove from heat.
3. Place cumin and oregano in a mortar bowl or spice grinder; grind using a pestle or grinder until mixture becomes a medium-fine powder.
4. Process peppers, spice mixture, orange juice, lime juice, brown sugar, Roasted Garlic, and ¹/₂ cup reserved water in a blender until smooth, stopping to scrape down sides as needed. Add table salt to taste.

Roasted Garlic

To roast garlic, preheat oven to 425°F. Cut off pointed end of 1 garlic head; place garlic on a piece of aluminum foil. Fold foil to seal. Bake at 425°F for 30 minutes; let cool 10 minutes. Squeeze pulp from garlic cloves.
Makes *2 Tbsp.*

BAKED MEXICAN RICE

My roommate in college was from Mexico City, and of the many recipes we shared, one of my favorites of hers was a simple rice preparation. Whole chunks of onion and garlic permeate the rice as it cooks and are removed right before serving for a simple side to complement any Tex-Mex dish.

Makes *4 cups* · **Hands-on** *10 min.* · **Total** *40 min.*

1 Tbsp. butter
1 medium onion, quartered
4 garlic cloves, crushed

1 cup uncooked long-grain rice
2 cups unsalted chicken broth
³/₄ tsp. table salt

1. Preheat oven to 350°F. Melt butter in a 3-qt. ovenproof saucepan over medium-high heat; add onion and garlic. Sauté 4 minutes or until tender, making sure onion wedges remain intact. Remove onion and garlic from saucepan, and set aside. Add rice to pan; cook, stirring constantly 2 minutes or until golden brown.
2. Stir in chicken broth and salt; add reserved onion and garlic to pan. Bring to a boil. Bake, covered, at 350°F for 25 minutes or until liquid is absorbed and rice is tender. Remove from oven, and let stand, covered, 5 minutes. Uncover, and remove and discard onion and garlic.

RED RICE (ARROZ ROJO)

Makes *4 cups* · **Hands-on** *10 min.* · **Total** *45 min.*

Prepare Baked Mexican Rice as directed through Step 1. Add 3 Tbsp. tomato paste to rice mixture; sauté 1 minute. Add 1 whole serrano pepper to saucepan with chicken broth. Proceed with recipe as directed. Top with chopped serrano pepper, if desired.

GREEN RICE (ARROZ VERDE)

Makes *4 ¹/₄ cups* · **Hands-on** *18 min.* · **Total** *48 min.*

Prepare Baked Mexican Rice as directed through Step 1. Process 1 cup loosely packed fresh cilantro leaves, 2 stemmed and seeded poblano peppers, and 1 cup unsalted chicken broth in a blender until smooth. Add cilantro mixture, ³/₄ cup unsalted chicken broth, and ³/₄ tsp. table salt to saucepan; stir to combine. Proceed with recipe as directed.

BLACK BEANS

Among the bean options in Tex-Mex restaurants, refried, charro, and borracho were the original selections, but around the mid-1990s, black beans began to creep onto menus across the state. For a complete meal, serve these legumes over Baked Mexican Rice (page 192) and top with a fried egg.

Makes *6 to 8 servings* · **Hands-on** *15 min.* · **Total** *45 min.*

3 plum tomatoes, halved
1 small onion, quartered
$^1/_2$ cup firmly packed fresh cilantro leaves
1 jalapeño pepper, seeded

1 garlic clove
$^1/_2$ tsp. kosher salt
2 (15-oz.) cans black beans, drained
1 Tbsp. olive oil

1. Pulse first 6 ingredients in a food processor until chunky.
2. Bring tomato mixture, beans, and oil to a boil in a medium saucepan; cover, reduce heat, and simmer, stirring occasionally, 30 minutes.

PECAN PRALINES

It's rare not to see flan, sopapillas (puffy pillows of fried flour tortillas drizzled with cinnamon and honey), and pralines on Tex-Mex restaurant menus. There's only one authentic style of Texas praline. It must be relatively flat, hard to the touch, and offer both a creamy and crispy sugar texture as it melts away on your palate. If you find someone peddling the chewy kind somewhere, it's not the authentic Texas thing.

Makes *1 ½ dozen* · **Hands-on** *20 min.* · **Total** *30 min.*

1 (16-oz.) package light brown sugar
1 (5-oz.) can evaporated milk
1 ½ cups pecan pieces

1 tsp. vanilla extract
Wax paper

1. Bring brown sugar and evaporated milk to a boil in a heavy 4-qt. saucepan over medium heat, stirring constantly. Boil, stirring occasionally, 4 to 6 minutes or until a candy thermometer registers 236°F (soft ball stage). Remove sugar mixture from heat.
2. Let sugar mixture stand until candy thermometer reaches 150°F (20 to 25 minutes). Stir in pecans and vanilla using a wooden spoon; stir constantly 1 to 2 minutes or just until mixture begins to lose its gloss.
3. Quickly drop by heaping tablespoonfuls onto wax paper, and let stand until firm (10 to 15 minutes).

COCONUT FLAN

A creamy, custardy dessert is hard to pass up, and this flan with flavors of coconut is no exception. Flan has particular sway for me for the slightly burnt flavor of the sugar that caramelizes in the bottom of the pan as it cooks.

Makes *8 servings* · **Hands-on** *25 min.* · **Total** *6 hours, 40 min.*

1 cup sugar
1 (13.66-oz.) can coconut milk
1 cup cream of coconut
1 cup sweetened condensed milk

1 tsp. vanilla extract
5 large eggs
Garnish: toasted coconut flakes

1. Preheat oven to 325°F. Combine sugar and ½ cup water in a heavy saucepan; cook over low heat 10 to 12 minutes or until sugar melts and turns a light golden brown. Remove from heat; immediately pour hot caramelized sugar into 8 (6-oz.) lightly greased ramekins. Let stand 6 minutes or until sugar hardens.
2. Whisk together coconut milk and next 4 ingredients in a large bowl until smooth. Pour mixture evenly over sugar in each ramekin. Place ramekins in a large roasting pan. Add hot tap water to pan to a depth of 1 inch. Cover loosely with aluminum foil.
3. Bake at 325°F for 55 minutes to 1 hour and 10 minutes or until slightly set. (Flan will jiggle when pan is shaken.) Remove ramekins from water bath; place on a wire rack. Cool completely (about 1 hour). Cover and chill at least 4 hours. Run a knife around edges of flans to loosen; invert flans onto serving plates.

COFFEE LIQUEUR CAKE

Kahlúa from just across the border flavors this rich cake spiked with brewed coffee. Be sure to measure the Bundt pan if you aren't sure of its size. Measure by pouring water from a liquid measuring cup to fill the pan. If you use a traditional 14-cup Bundt pan, adjust the bake time to 40 minutes or until a long wooden pick inserted in center comes out clean.

Makes *10 servings* · **Hands-on** *15 min.* · **Total** *3 hours, including glaze*

1 ³/₄ cups all-purpose flour
1 cup granulated sugar
1 cup firmly packed brown sugar
³/₄ cup unsweetened cocoa
1 tsp. baking soda
1 tsp. baking powder

³/₄ tsp. table salt
1 cup vegetable oil
³/₄ cup brewed coffee, at room temperature
¹/₂ cup coffee liqueur, such as Kahlúa
4 large eggs
Coffee Glaze (recipe follows)

1. Preheat oven to 350°F.
2. Combine first 7 ingredients in a large bowl. Stir together oil and next 3 ingredients in another bowl. Add oil mixture to flour mixture, whisking until blended. Pour batter into a greased and floured 10-inch (14-cup) Bundt pan.
3. Bake at 350°F for 50 minutes or until a long wooden pick inserted in center comes out clean. Cool in pan on a wire rack 15 minutes; remove from pan to wire rack, and cool completely (about 1 ¹/₂ hours).
4. Prepare glaze, and immediately spoon over cake.

COFFEE GLAZE

Makes *³/₄ cup* · **Hands-on** *10 min.* · **Total** *10 min.*

1 oz. unsweetened chocolate, chopped
3 Tbsp. butter
1 cup powdered sugar

1 Tbsp. milk
1 Tbsp. coffee liqueur, such as Kahlúa

Cook chocolate and butter in a small saucepan over medium heat, stirring constantly, until chocolate and butter melt. Remove from heat. Beat in powdered sugar, milk, and liqueur, whisking until smooth.

CINNAMON ICE CREAM

When serving chocolate desserts, ice cream is always a welcome addition. Cinnamon and chocolate are always wonderful together and are a common flavor combination from south of the border.

Makes *3 cups* · **Hands-on** *15 min.* · **Total** *6 hours, 45 min.*

¹/₂ vanilla bean	4 large egg yolks
1 ³/₄ cups milk	¹/₄ tsp. ground cinnamon
¹/₂ cup sugar	

1. Split vanilla bean lengthwise, and scrape out seeds. Cook milk, vanilla bean, and seeds in a heavy nonaluminum saucepan over medium heat, stirring often, 6 minutes or just until bubbles appear (do not boil); remove from heat.
2. Whisk together sugar and egg yolks in a medium bowl until thick and pale. Gradually whisk in about ¹/₂ cup hot milk mixture into yolks. Add yolk mixture to remaining hot milk mixture, whisking constantly. Cook over medium-low heat, whisking constantly, 2 minutes or until mixture thickens and coats a spoon. (Do not boil.) Remove from heat; pour through a fine wire-mesh strainer into a bowl. Whisk in cinnamon, and let stand 30 minutes. Cover and chill 4 hours.
3. Pour mixture into freezer container of a 1 ¹/₂-qt. electric ice-cream maker, and freeze according to manufacturer's instructions. (Instructions and times may vary.)

CHAPTER FIVE

WEST ★ TEXAS ★

West Texas is home to expansive grassy plains with long stretches of barbed-wire delineating hundreds of thousands of acres of cattle ranches. The area was settled after the Civil War when the buffalo no longer roamed, the Comanches were relocated to reservations, and westward expansion of the United States began in the form of cattle drives. The region is known for a subtle, yet rich layer of Mexican flavor that melds with frontier-style cooking to deliver an altogether different cuisine from South Texas' Tex-Mex.

TEXAS CAVIAR

Before 1940, it's doubtful anyone would have elevated the humble black-eyed pea to the status of caviar, but Helen Corbitt changed that. A native New Yorker, she came to Texas to be a catering teacher at the University of Texas. She eventually moved on to become catering director at the Houston Country Club, the historic Driskill Hotel in Austin, and the Zodiac Room at Neiman Marcus, where many of her recipes remain on the menu today. Among her most famous innovations is Texas Caviar, a veritable salad of pickled black-eyed peas and other vegetables that unwittingly became one of the state's most popular party dishes. Serve it as an appetizer with tortilla chips or as a side dish for grilled chicken or beef. Chilling not only makes the recipe a convenient prep-ahead dish, it allows the flavors to develop.

Makes *7 to 8 cups* · **Hands-on** *15 min.* · **Total** *15 min., plus 8 hours chill time*

2 (15-oz.) cans black-eyed peas, drained
    and rinsed
2 plum tomatoes, diced
2 green onions, chopped
1 cup fresh corn kernels (2 ears)*

¹/₂ cup chopped red bell pepper
¹/₂ cup Salsa Fresca (page 150)
¹/₄ cup chopped fresh cilantro
2 garlic cloves, minced
1 tsp. table salt

Stir together all ingredients in a serving bowl. Cover and chill, stirring occasionally, 8 hours.

*1 (8-oz.) can whole kernel corn, drained, may be substituted for fresh corn kernels.

RAJAS CON QUESO

A cheesier twist on the classic Mexican dish Rajas con Crema,
or Mexican cream, this recipe is one of the many ways to make
a really great chile con queso. The flavor and velvety texture of
sautéed poblano peppers and vegetables added to the melted cheese
is addictive and should be served with sturdy tortilla chips or with
a side of warm tortillas for dipping.

Makes *3 1/2 cups* · **Hands-on** *35 min.* · **Total** *45 min.*

2 lb. poblano peppers
1 cup thinly sliced white onion
1 garlic clove, minced
Pinch of table salt
2 tsp. vegetable or corn oil
3/4 cup milk
1 Tbsp. cornstarch

3 Tbsp. crema or sour cream
1 1/2 cups (6 oz.) shredded Monterey Jack
or quesadilla cheese
1 cup (4 oz.) shredded deli white American
cheese
Tortilla chips

1. Preheat broiler. Broil peppers on an aluminum foil-lined baking sheet 5 inches from heat 12 to 15 minutes or until peppers look blistered.
2. Place peppers in a large zip-top plastic freezer bag; seal and let stand 10 to 15 minutes to loosen skins. Peel peppers; remove and discard seeds. Cut peppers into strips.
3. Sauté onion, garlic, and salt in hot oil in a medium skillet over medium heat 8 minutes or until tender. Stir in pepper strips.
4. Combine milk and cornstarch in a small bowl, stirring until smooth. Add milk mixture to skillet. Bring to a light boil. Remove from heat; add crema and cheeses, stirring until cheese is melted and mixture is creamy. Season with salt and pepper to taste. Serve immediately with tortilla chips.

HUEVOS RANCHEROS

Literally translated as "rancher's eggs," this breakfast dish originated on the tables of Mexican farms where fresh farm eggs were fried up and served over corn tortillas with red chile sauce and refried beans. The modern Texas version isn't much different. Serve it with your favorite salsa if you'd like, or use the fresh salsa suggested here, where the brightness of flavor melds well with the creaminess of the fried egg yolk.

Makes *4 servings* · **Hands-on** *30 min.* · **Total** *30 min.*

1 1/2 cups chopped onion
1 Tbsp. canola oil
2 garlic cloves, minced
4 1/2 cups chopped tomatoes
1 Tbsp. white vinegar
2 tsp. sugar
1 tsp. ground cumin
1/2 tsp. table salt
1 (4-oz.) can chopped green chiles
1 medium-size green bell pepper, chopped
1 jalapeño pepper, seeded and minced

1/2 cup firmly packed fresh cilantro, chopped
2 Tbsp. fresh lime juice
Canola oil
8 (6-inch) corn tortillas
8 large eggs
1/4 cup crema or sour cream
1/2 cup (2 oz.) shredded Mexican four-cheese blend
2 medium-size ripe avocados, sliced
Lime wedges

1. Sauté onion in 1 Tbsp. hot oil in large nonstick skillet over medium-high heat about 3 minutes or until just set. Add garlic; sauté 1 minute. Stir in tomatoes and next 7 ingredients. Bring to a light boil; reduce heat to medium, and simmer, stirring occasionally, 15 minutes. Remove from heat, and let cool to room temperature. Stir in cilantro and lime juice. Cover and chill until ready to serve.
2. Pour oil to depth of about 1/2 inch into a 12-inch skillet; heat to 350°F. Fry tortillas, in batches, 10 seconds on each side or until tortillas are crisp on the edges but tender in the centers. Drain on paper towels.
3. Remove oil from skillet, reserving just enough in skillet to coat bottom. Place skillet over low heat. Gently break 4 eggs into hot skillet. Cook 2 to 3 minutes on each side or to desired degree of doneness. Remove eggs from skillet; keep warm. Repeat procedure with remaining eggs.
4. Place 2 tortillas on each of 4 plates. Top each tortilla with about 1/2 cup salsa, avocado slices, 1 fried egg, crema, and cheese. Serve with lime wedges.

FRONTIER BREAKFAST TACOS

Perhaps almost more popular than the regular taco, breakfast tacos seem to be the driving force behind what gets many Texans up and going in the morning. It doesn't take a rocket scientist to see the brilliance behind wrapping a classic American breakfast of eggs, bacon, and potatoes in a tortilla to go. In truth, there's nothing authentically Mexican about a breakfast taco. It's absolutely an adaptation that has found a happy place on breakfast menus throughout Texas.

Makes *4 servings* · **Hands-on** *35 min.* · **Total** *35 min.*

1 cup frozen shredded hash browns
¼ cup canola oil
4 hickory-smoked bacon slices
⅓ cup thinly sliced green onions
8 large eggs, lightly beaten

1 cup (4 oz.) shredded Mexican four-cheese blend
8 (6-inch) flour tortillas, warmed
Salsa Fresca (page 150)

1. Prepare hash browns according to package directions, using ¼ cup canola oil. Drain on paper towels.

2. Cook bacon in a large skillet over medium-low heat 8 minutes or until crisp; remove bacon, and drain on paper towels, reserving 2 Tbsp. drippings in skillet. Coarsely crumble bacon.

3. Sauté green onions in hot drippings in skillet over medium-high heat 1 minute or until tender. Add eggs to skillet, and cook, without stirring, 1 to 2 minutes or until eggs begin to set on bottom. Gently draw cooked edges away from sides of skillet to form large pieces. Cook, stirring occasionally, 1 to 2 minutes or until eggs are thickened and moist. (Do not overstir.) Add hash browns and bacon, stirring gently just until combined. Sprinkle with cheese; remove from heat, and let stand 1 minute or until cheese is melted.

4. Divide egg mixture among warm tortillas. Top with Salsa Fresca. Roll up each tortilla, and serve immediately.

WEST TEXAS CHILI

Native Americans rubbed dried meat with smashed chiles to pack in saddle bags for travel—a method adopted by frontiersmen. The meat and chiles later were cooked with water over the campfire to make a hot meal. Texans consider beans a Yankee addition from north of the Red River—keep them out of the chili.

Makes *8 servings* · **Hands-on** *35 min.* · **Total** *1 hour, 35 min.*

2 large onions, diced
1/4 cup vegetable or canola oil
5 garlic cloves, finely minced
2 lb. ground chuck or venison
1 Tbsp. table salt
3 Tbsp. ancho chile powder
2 Tbsp. ground cumin

1 Tbsp. paprika
2 (14.5-oz.) cans diced tomatoes
1 (6-oz.) can tomato paste
1 (12-oz.) can amber ale beer
2 Tbsp. masa harina (corn flour)
1 (16-oz.) can pinto beans, drained and
   rinsed (optional; see note above)

1. Sauté onions in hot oil in a large Dutch oven or stockpot over medium-high heat 7 minutes or until translucent. Add garlic, and sauté 1 minute. Add beef, and cook, stirring often, 6 minutes or until meat crumbles and is no longer pink. Drain, reserving 2 Tbsp. drippings in Dutch oven; return beef to Dutch oven.
2. Stir in salt and next 3 ingredients; cook 2 minutes. Stir in tomatoes and tomato paste.
3. Add 3/4 cup beer and 1 cup water; simmer 20 minutes, stirring occasionally. Add remaining 3/4 cup beer and 1/2 cup water; simmer 30 minutes, stirring occasionally.
4. Add masa; cook 10 minutes. Add additional water to reach desired consistency.

FRITO PIE

A staple of Friday night football games, the Frito pie is a small bag of Fritos slit open and ladled with Texas chili and a choice of garnishes.

Makes *8 servings* · **Hands-on** *15 min.* · **Total** *15 min.*

8 cups Fritos® original corn chips
8 cups warm West Texas Chili
2 cups (8 oz.) shredded sharp Cheddar
   cheese

1/2 cup diced white onion
Toppings: sour cream, sliced fresh
   jalapeño peppers

Place 1 cup chips into each of 8 bowls. Ladle 1 cup West Texas Chili on top of corn chips in each bowl. Sprinkle each with 1/4 cup cheese and 1 Tbsp. onion. Top with desired toppings.

PORK AND BLACK BEAN "STEW"

Roasted Tomato and Ancho Salsa and Peach Preserves add sweet heat to this stew. If you like beans in your chili, consider this a Texas nod to "American-style" chili with beans, only with uncommon flavors.

Makes *4 to 6 servings* · **Hands-on** *25 min.* · **Total** *25 min.*

1 (1 ½-lb.) pork tenderloin, cut in
    ½-inch cubes
2 Tbsp. Texas Meat Rub (page 13)
2 Tbsp. olive oil
1 cup Roasted Tomato and Ancho Salsa
    (page 153)

¼ cup Peach Preserves (recipe follows)
1 (15-oz.) can black beans, drained
    and rinsed
¾ cup chicken broth

1. Sprinkle pork with Texas Meat Rub, and toss well to coat.
2. Cook pork in hot oil in a large skillet over medium-high heat, stirring occasionally, 5 minutes or until browned on all sides. Add salsa, preserves, beans, and broth. Simmer 5 minutes or until pork is tender and sauce is thickened.

PEACH PRESERVES

Makes *10 (8-oz.) jars* · **Hands-on** *50 min.* · **Total** *1 hour, 5 min.*

12 fresh peaches, peeled and chopped*
4 ½ cups sugar
1 Tbsp. firmly packed lemon zest

2 tsp. fresh lemon juice
1 (1 ¾-oz.) package powdered pectin

1. Crush 1 cup peaches in a large saucepan. Add remaining peaches, and bring to a low boil. Cook, stirring occasionally, until peaches become translucent and a candy thermometer registers 220°F (about 20 minutes).
2. Add sugar and next 2 ingredients, and return to a boil over medium heat. Gradually stir in pectin, and boil 1 minute. Skim foam from top of liquid, and discard. Remove from heat.
3. Spoon mixture into 10 (8-oz.) hot sterilized jars, filling to ¼ inch from top; wipe jar rims clean. Cover at once with metal lids, and screw on bands. Process jars in boiling-water bath 15 minutes. Let cool before storing in a cool, dark place up to 1 year. Refrigerate after opening.

*12 cups frozen peaches may be substituted.

RED CHILE PORK POSOLE

Posole is a common Mexican hominy-based soup made from dried corn that has been soaked in a solution of lye, slaked lime, or wood ash—a process called nixtamalization, which makes the corn more nutritious and shelf stable. This is inspired by Chef Lou Lambert of Lamberts Downtown Barbecue in Austin.

Makes *8 servings* · **Hands-on** *50 min.* · **Total** *2 hours, 50 min.*

3 dried ancho chile peppers (about
   1 ¼ oz.), seeded and coarsely chopped
1 plum tomato, coarsely chopped
1 cup chicken broth
½ cup coarsely chopped yellow onion
1 Tbsp. apple cider vinegar
2 garlic cloves
1 tsp. ground cumin
2 lb. boneless pork shoulder roast
   (Boston butt), trimmed and cut into
   1-inch cubes
1 tsp. kosher salt
1 tsp. freshly ground black pepper
2 Tbsp. vegetable oil

1 large onion, diced
6 garlic cloves, minced
¼ cup coarsely chopped fresh cilantro
1 tsp. sugar
1 tsp. ground cumin
½ tsp. dried oregano
3 bay leaves
1 (28-oz.) can diced tomatoes, drained
1 (32-oz.) container chicken broth
2 (15-oz.) cans white hominy, drained
   and rinsed
Toppings: thinly sliced cabbage, chopped
   white onion, sliced radishes, chopped
   avocado, lime wedges

1. Bring ancho chile peppers and next 6 ingredients and a pinch of salt and pepper to a simmer in a small saucepan; cook 2 minutes. Cover, remove from heat, and let stand 15 minutes.
2. Process ancho chile pepper mixture in a blender until smooth, stopping to scrape down sides as needed; set aside.
3. Sprinkle pork with salt and pepper. Sauté pork in hot oil in a large Dutch oven over medium-high heat, stirring constantly, 6 minutes or until browned. Add onion, and sauté 3 minutes or until tender. Add garlic, and cook 1 minute or until garlic just begins to brown.
4. Stir in the ancho chile puree and next 5 ingredients. Cook, stirring often, 2 minutes. Add tomatoes, broth, and hominy. Bring to a boil; reduce heat to low and simmer, uncovered, stirring occasionally, 1 hour. Partially cover, and simmer 30 to 45 minutes or until pork is tender and mixture is slightly thickened. Remove and discard bay leaves. Serve with desired toppings.

TEXAS TOOLS

Molino

The likelihood that you'll take up grinding corn as a pastime is fairly slim, but just the same, you can't do much better than with a hand-cranked corn grinder or molino. When dried hominy is ground, the resulting product is masa seca or masa harina, which is the common ingredient for tamales and corn tortillas.

GREEN CHILE PORK STEW

Many people think that Green Chile Pork Stew belongs only in New Mexico, but because of the heavy influences of the green chile found in West Texas, it is a classic in this part of the state. The stew freezes well, so make a big batch to enjoy some now and later.

Makes *6 servings* · **Hands-on** *30 min.* · **Total** *2 hours, 50 min.*

TEXAS TIDBIT
___

THE LONG GREEN CHILE

Tex-Mex on this side of the state is more heavily influenced by one particular chile: the green chile. Referred to by a number of synonyms including Anaheim chile, New Mexico chile, long green chile, Hatch chile, and sometimes Chimayo chile—all of which are slightly different from one another—the distinctive green chile is the primary chile ingredient for sauces, soups, and chile powders in these parts.

1 lb. tomatillos, husks removed
1/2 lb. fresh Hatch chile peppers*
1 1/2 tsp. table salt, divided
1 onion, chopped
1 (32-oz.) container chicken broth
1 cup firmly packed fresh cilantro leaves
2 Tbsp. fresh lime juice
2 tsp. Worcestershire sauce
3 garlic cloves, chopped

2 1/2 lb. boneless pork shoulder roast (Boston butt), trimmed and cut into 1-inch pieces
1 tsp. freshly ground black pepper
3 Tbsp. vegetable oil
Tortilla chips, flour tortillas, or Skillet Cornbread (page 88)
Garnishes: fresh cilantro, julienned radishes

1. Preheat broiler. Cut tomatillos into large chunks; set aside.
2. Broil peppers on an aluminum foil-lined baking sheet 5 inches from heat 3 to 4 minutes on each side or until peppers look blistered. Place peppers in a large zip-top plastic freezer bag; seal and let stand 10 minutes to loosen skins. Peel peppers; remove and discard seeds.
3. Bring tomatillos, Hatch peppers, 1/2 tsp. salt, onion, and next 5 ingredients to a light boil in a large saucepan; remove from heat, and cool slightly.
4. Process tomatillo mixture, in batches, in a blender until smooth, stopping to scrape down sides as needed (or use a handheld immersion blender, if desired).
5. Sprinkle pork with remaining 1 tsp. salt and pepper. Sauté pork, in batches, in hot oil in a Dutch oven over medium-high heat, stirring often, 4 minutes or until browned.
6. Add tomatillo mixture to Dutch oven, stirring to loosen browned bits from bottom of Dutch oven. Bring to a light simmer; cover, reduce heat to medium-low, and simmer, stirring occasionally, 1 1/2 hours or until pork is fork-tender. Uncover and cook, stirring occasionally, 30 minutes or until liquid is slightly thickened. Serve with flour tortillas or Skillet Cornbread.

*3 (4-oz.) cans Hatch green chile peppers may be substituted for fresh Hatch chile peppers. Skip Steps 2 and 3.

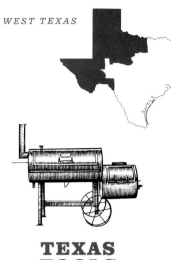

SMOKED CHICKEN

Smoked chicken is great on its own served with a good barbecue sauce and any number of side dishes, but if you're going to go to the trouble of firing up the smoker, it makes sense to smoke 4 to 5 chickens at once. Once the chickens are done, debone them and use the meat in enchiladas, tortilla soup, or in King Ranch Chicken (page 168).

Makes *12 servings* · **Hands-on** *15 min.* · **Total** *4 hours, 5 min.*

3 to 4 oak, hickory, or pecan wood chunks
1 cup firmly packed piloncillo (Mexican
    brown sugar) (about 1 [8-oz.] cone)*
1 Tbsp. ancho chile powder

1 Tbsp. table salt
1 Tbsp. freshly ground black pepper
4 (3 ³/₄- to 4-lb.) whole chickens

1. Soak wood chunks in water to cover 1 hour.
2. Meanwhile, combine piloncillo and next 3 ingredients in a small bowl. Rub chickens with piloncillo mixture, and let stand 30 minutes.
3. Prepare smoker according to manufacturer's directions. Place water pan in smoker; add water to depth of fill line. Bring internal temperature to 225° to 250°F and maintain temperature 15 to 20 minutes.
4. Drain wood chunks, and place on coals. Place chickens on food cooking grate; close smoker. Smoke 2 ¹/₂ to 3 hours or until a meat thermometer inserted into thickest portion of thighs registers 165°F.
5. Remove chickens from smoker, and let stand 20 minutes before slicing.

Note: Piloncillo is a raw sugar made from reduced cane juice. It's sold molded into cone shapes and is sometimes labeled panela. To measure, place the cone in a zip-top plastic freezer bag, and pound it with a meat mallet to break it apart.

*Dark brown sugar may be substituted for piloncillo.

SMOKED TURKEY

For a 10- to 12-lb. turkey, season as directed and increase the cooking time to 3 ¹/₂ to 4 hours or until a meat thermometer inserted into the thickest portion of the thigh registers 165°F.

TEXAS TOOLS

Offset Smoker

If you're gonna make barbecue in Texas, you've gotta have an offset smoker. You can get by with a grill setup and cook with indirect heat, but the truth is, you'll never duplicate the kind of barbecue of Texas legend. The result of this style of cooking brings two distinctive qualities to barbecue, namely red smoke rings and crisp bark (crust) on perfectly cooked Texas brisket. An offset smoker has a barrel cook chamber for the meat and a firebox on the side or back for the wood. A fire is built with kindling or lump charcoal with the air intake vent and charcoal vent fully open. The portal between the firebox and the cook chamber transports the smoke that exits through a chimney. Heat is controlled by the amount of wood and oxygen brought in through the air intake and the exhaust vents.

TOM PERINI

CHUCKWAGON COOK/RESTAURATEUR, PERINI RANCH
STEAKHOUSE, BUFFALO GAP

Spend a few days with Tom Perini on his ranch in Buffalo Gap and you'll find a man as rooted in the rough-hewn Western soils of the Callahan Divide escarpment as any of the old gnarly mesquite trees and live oaks scattered throughout the sun-parched region.

The Perini family has been ranching since Tom was a boy in the 1950s. At age 22, he became an official cattleman for the family ranch following his father's passing. During that time, he developed a passion for chuck wagon cooking, and he eventually transformed the ranch's hay barn into the rustic Perini Ranch Steakhouse in 1983.

In the early days of cattle drives, the chuckwagon was the mobile kitchen. With no option for refrigeration and no fresh gardens to peruse for vegetables, beans and beef were the only food options that could sustain a long trip. Along the trail, ranchers would slaughter a steer and hang the carcass on the side of the wagon at night to chill it down as much as possible. The next morning, they'd wrap it up with tarps and put it in the wagon with blankets to maintain the cool temperature.

A modern-day chuckwagon comes in the form of a pick-up truck with ample cooler storage and plenty of additional amenities for cooking a wider range of food. From the late 1800s all the way to modern-day ranching, the common thread in cowboy cooking has always been one thing: fire.

"When you get a good piece of beef, season it with a little rub and cook it over a mesquite flame. All of a sudden, you have something magical," says Perini, who does all of his flame cooking with aged mesquite wood—the most common wood found in West Texas. "It's the smoke and flame that make it great. That's the way a steak ought to be."

The restaurant menu includes everything from whole pit-roasted prime rib; flame-seared bone-in rib eye rubbed with salt, garlic, and pepper; green chile hominy; and classic Southern-style green beans. Perini believes it's about preserving a part of Texas food culture.

"A lot of people these days think a barbecue is going out on the back porch and cooking a weenie with a gas grill and some wood chips. That's not barbecue. There's something about an open flame and cast iron and all the little flavors that come together that mean something a lot more than that. Preserving these methods of cooking is important because we want people to remember where they come from when they eat here."

With his heart set on preserving a Texas way of life through his food, he invites anyone to try a little pit cooking of their own at home. Just be sure to do it right. You could use a gas grill and a bag of wood chips and call it Texas cooking, but you'd be wrong, at least if Tom Perini has anything to say about it.

"It's the smoke and flame that make it great. That's the way a steak ought to be."

PERINI RANCH LAREDO BROIL

TEXAS TIDBIT

RIDING AND ROPING— THE COWBOY WAY

Herding cattle meant long days—and nights—of riding and roping. But in the moments of free time afforded the hardworking cowboys and vaqueros, they always made time to ride and rope some more. In open fields, they created competitions racing their horses and performing rope tricks, all in an effort to determine the best of the crew. These were the early days of barrel racing, steer wrestling, calf roping, and bronco riding.

In the early 1930s, the crowds and fanfare for the competitive cowboy antics formally culminated in the beginning of the American rodeo circuit, a vibrantly competitive collection of events that still thrives throughout the country today.

The London broil often plays second fiddle to standard steak cuts, but it's a flavorful, inexpensive cut of meat to grill for a party. This version from Perini Ranch Steakhouse is a nice, spicy alternative to the average Sunday roast. Serve it with baked potatoes and grilled asparagus, and you've got a great family-style meal.

Makes *6 to 8 servings* · **Hands-on** *15 min.* **Total** *1 hour, 5 min., plus 24 hours marinating*

1 ½ cups dry red wine
½ cup soy sauce
3 Tbsp. Worcestershire sauce
6 garlic cloves, minced
1 Tbsp. dry mustard
3 Tbsp. freshly ground black pepper, divided

2 ½ to 3 lb. London broil
1 Tbsp. dried oregano
1 Tbsp. paprika
2 tsp. celery salt
½ tsp. ground red pepper

1. Stir together first 5 ingredients and 1 Tbsp. black pepper in a shallow dish or large zip-top plastic freezer bag; add London broil. Cover or seal, and chill 24 hours. Remove from marinade, discarding marinade.
2. Preheat grill to 300° to 350°F (medium) heat. Stir together oregano, next 3 ingredients, and remaining 2 Tbsp. black pepper; rub over London broil. Let stand 15 to 20 minutes.
3. Grill, covered with grill lid, 12 to 15 minutes on each side or to desired degree of doneness. Let stand 10 minutes. Cut diagonally across the grain into thin strips.

PERINI RANCH ROASTED PRIME RIB

The holiday sideboard standard doesn't have to be intimidating to prepare. This recipe requires a simple rub and roast. Starting it in a blasting hot oven helps develop a crusty exterior, while cooking at a lower temp to perfection ensures it remains tender and juicy and the marbled fat melts into the meat without burning.

Makes *12 servings* · **Hands-on** *15 min.* · **Total** *3 hours, 10 min., including sauce*

1/2 cup coarsely ground black pepper
1/4 cup kosher salt
2 Tbsp. all-purpose flour
2 Tbsp. garlic powder

2 Tbsp. dried oregano
1 (11-lb.) boneless prime rib roast, trimmed
Perini Ranch Horseradish Sauce

1. Preheat oven to 500°F.
2. Stir together first 5 ingredients until well blended. Coat prime rib with rub, and let stand 30 minutes.
3. Place roast on a rack in a roasting pan.
4. Bake at 500°F for 15 minutes. Reduce heat to 325°F, and bake 2 hours and 20 minutes or to desired degree of doneness. Cover loosely with aluminum foil, and let stand 15 minutes before slicing. Serve with Perini Ranch Horseradish Sauce.

PERINI RANCH HORSERADISH SAUCE

Fresh parsley adds lively flavor and a pop of color to a classic.

Makes *1 1/4 cups* · **Hands-on** *5 min.* · **Total** *5 min.*

1 cup sour cream
3 Tbsp. prepared horseradish

2 tsp. finely chopped fresh parsley

Stir together all ingredients in a small bowl. Add salt and pepper to taste. Refrigerate in airtight container for up to 5 days.

CARNE GUISADA

Carne Guisada is a dish that relies on hands-off, low and slow cooking. Like any classic braise, the meat becomes more tender and the flavors more concentrated with time and patience. The aromas alone from this slow-cooked stew will make it hard to wait until serving time. This is a perfect make-ahead dish for entertaining friends and can be served as you would chili or as a taco filling with your favorite toppings.

Makes *6 servings* · **Hands-on** *30 min.* · **Total** *3 hours*

¹/₄ cup all-purpose flour
1 tsp. table salt
1 tsp. freshly ground black pepper
3 lb. boneless chuck roast, trimmed and
  cut into 1-inch pieces
2 Tbsp. vegetable oil
2 medium onions, chopped
3 celery ribs, chopped
4 jalapeño peppers, seeded and minced
2 Tbsp. tomato paste

3 cups beef broth
2 ¹/₄ cups beer, such as Shiner Bock
4 tsp. ground cumin
1 Tbsp. chili powder
Corn or flour tortillas
"Ninfa's" Green Sauce (page 151)
Toppings: chopped green onions, chopped
  fresh cilantro, sour cream, sliced red
  jalapeños

1. Preheat oven to 350°F. Combine flour, salt, and pepper in a shallow dish; toss beef with flour mixture.

2. Cook beef, in batches, in hot oil in a large Dutch oven over medium-high heat, stirring occasionally, 4 minutes or until browned. Remove beef from Dutch oven.

3. Add onion, celery, and jalapeño peppers to Dutch oven; sauté 5 minutes or until tender. Stir in any remaining flour mixture and tomato paste; cook 2 minutes. Add broth, next 3 ingredients, and beef, stirring to loosen browned bits from bottom of Dutch oven. Bring to a light boil.

4. Bake, covered, at 350°F for 2 ¹/₂ hours or until meat is fork-tender. Skim fat from juices in Dutch oven. Serve with "Ninfa's" Green Sauce and desired toppings.

TEXAS BURGERS

There's really no secret to grilling a great Texas-style burger. Start with ground chuck that is 20 percent fat, round out a few quarter-pound patties by hand—making sure not to compress the meat too much—sprinkle with salt and pepper, and grill them over a hot charcoal flame. To serve them in keeping with a tradition started by Texas-based fast-food chain, Whataburger, add a smear of classic yellow mustard. Jalapeños are also a Texas must, whether pickled or fresh.

Makes *4 servings* · **Hands-on** *20 min.* · **Total** *40 min.*

1 ½ lb. ground chuck
2 Tbsp. Worcestershire sauce
1 Tbsp. Texas Meat Rub (page 13)
4 (³/₄-oz.) slices longhorn-style Cheddar cheese*

1 medium jalapeño pepper, thinly sliced
4 hamburger buns
¼ cup butter, softened
Toppings: coarse-grained mustard, leaf lettuce, tomato slices, red onion slices

1. Preheat grill to 350° to 400°F (medium-high) heat. Shape ground chuck into 4 (4-inch) patties. Drizzle patties with Worcestershire sauce, and sprinkle with Texas Meat Rub. Let stand 15 minutes.
2. Grill patties, covered with grill lid, 2 to 3 minutes on each side or to desired degree of doneness; top with cheese. Grill, covered with grill lid, until cheese melts. Remove from grill; top with jalapeño, and let stand 5 minutes.
3. Butter buns, and toast on grill. Serve patties on toasted buns with desired toppings.

*Mild Cheddar or Colby cheese may be substituted for longhorn-style cheese.

TEXAS PIT STOPS

BUDDY'S DRIVE IN
Andrews

THE BIG TEXAN STEAK RANCH
Amarillo

JOE T. GARCIAS'S
Fort Worth

DUTCH'S HAMBURGERS
Fort Worth

H&H CARWASH AND COFFEE SHOP
El Paso

MARY'S CAFE
Strawn

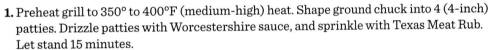

ADOBO GRILLED BEEF RIB EYES

Adobo sauce, made of spices, sesame, raisins, and chiles, adds robust flavor to beefy rib eyes, while a perky green chile salsa verde in the style of Ojinaga, Mexico, a town just across the Texas border, adds brightness and cuts the fattiness of the meat.

Makes *6 servings* · **Hands-on** *1 hour, 40 min.* · **Total** *4 hours*

TEXAS TIDBIT

FORT WORTH STOCKYARDS

GREEN CHILE SALSA VERDE
1 large poblano pepper
1 serrano pepper, seeded and finely
    chopped
$^1/_2$ cup chopped shallots (about 2 large)
$^1/_2$ cup red wine vinegar
$^1/_2$ cup olive oil
$^1/_4$ cup chopped fresh flat-leaf parsley
$^1/_4$ cup chopped fresh cilantro
2 green onions, thinly sliced
1 garlic clove, minced
1 tsp. sugar

6 (12-oz.) rib-eye steaks ($^3/_4$ inch thick)
1 $^1/_4$ tsp. kosher salt
1 $^1/_4$ tsp. freshly ground black pepper
$^1/_4$ cup unsalted butter

ADOBO SAUCE
2 cups chicken broth
1 plum tomato, chopped
$^1/_2$ cup diced onion
2 garlic cloves, coarsely chopped
1 Tbsp. sesame seeds
1 Tbsp. light brown sugar
1 Tbsp. raisins
1 tsp. kosher salt
1 tsp. ground cumin
$^1/_2$ tsp. ground cinnamon
$^1/_2$ tsp. freshly ground black pepper
4 large dried ancho chile peppers,
    stemmed and seeded
2 small dried guajillo peppers, stemmed
    and seeded
1 Tbsp. apple cider vinegar

Following the completion of the railroads in the late 1870s, the need for long cattle drives from Texas ranches across the various regions of the country became an obsolete endeavor. Instead, trade for cattle came to a centralized spot in Fort Worth, which became the trading point for the whole northwest region of Texas. With the opening of the Fort Worth Union Stockyards, the Fort Worth Dressed Meat and Packing Company, and the creation of a few packing houses by the Swift and Armour companies in the 1890s, Fort Worth had officially earned its reputation as a cowtown. The stockyards served as a place where cattle, sheep, and hogs could be bought, sold, and slaughtered, and served as a major part of the cattle industry through the 1950s.

1. Prepare Green Chile Salsa Verde: Preheat broiler. Broil poblano pepper on an aluminum foil-lined baking sheet 3 inches from heat 8 minutes or until pepper looks blistered, turning after 4 minutes. Place in a zip-top plastic freezer bag; seal and let stand 10 minutes to loosen skin. Peel; remove and discard seeds. Finely chop pepper.
2. Stir together poblano pepper, serrano pepper, and remaining ingredients in a bowl. Let stand at least 1 hour before serving. Add salt and freshly ground black pepper to taste. (Refrigerate in airtight container up to 5 days.)
3. Prepare Adobo Sauce: Combine chicken broth and next 10 ingredients in a medium saucepan over low heat; cook 2 minutes. Cover, remove from heat, and let stand 15 minutes. Process broth mixture and peppers in a blender until smooth, scraping down sides as needed. Transfer sauce to a bowl, and stir in vinegar.
4. Season steaks; brush both sides with 1 cup adobo sauce. Cover and chill 1 to 2 hours.
5. Remove steaks from refrigerator, and let stand at room temperature 20 minutes.
6. Preheat grill to 350° to 400°F (medium-high) heat. Grill steaks, covered with grill lid, 7 to 8 minutes on each side or to desired degree of doneness. Let stand 10 minutes before serving.
7. Meanwhile, bring remaining Adobo Sauce to a simmer in a saucepan over low heat; add butter, 1 Tbsp. at a time, whisking until blended. Serve with steaks and Green Chile Salsa Verde.

SMOKED BEEF TENDERLOIN

If there's one thing Texans aren't afraid to do, it's putting something in a smoker. More than a simple pastime, it's nearly a rite of passage to christen and season a new smoker. Though the protein of choice usually varies, the tendency is to smoke big portions of meat—the larger the better. This smoked beef tenderloin is a special treat and ideal for family holiday dinners.

Makes *12 to 16 servings* · **Hands-on** *20 min.* · **Total** *3 hours, 10 min., including rub*

¼ cup firmly packed light brown sugar
¼ cup seasoned salt
2 Tbsp. kosher salt
3 Tbsp. Texas Meat Rub (page 13)
2 Tbsp. garlic powder

2 Tbsp. ancho chile powder
2 Tbsp. cracked black pepper
1 (7- to 8-lb.) beef tenderloin, trimmed
3 applewood chunks

1. Stir together first 7 ingredients; rub 1 cup brown sugar mixture over tenderloin. Reserve remaining brown sugar mixture for another use. Cover tenderloin, and let stand at room temperature for 1 hour.
2. Meanwhile, soak wood chunks in water 30 minutes. Prepare smoker according to manufacturer's directions, bringing internal temperature to 225° to 250°F; maintain temperature for 15 to 20 minutes.
3. Drain wood chunks, and place on hot coals. Cover with smoker lid, and let stand 5 minutes or until wood chunks begin to smoke. Place tenderloin on cooking grate; cover with smoker lid.
4. Smoke tenderloin, maintaining temperature inside smoker between 225° and 250°F, for 1 hour and 15 minutes or until a meat thermometer inserted into thickest portion registers 135°F or to desired degree of doneness.
5. Remove from grill. Cover loosely with aluminum foil, and let stand 15 minutes. Cut across the grain into thin slices.

LOU LAMBERT

CHEF/RESTAURATEUR, LAMBERTS DOWNTOWN BARBECUE
AUSTIN, LAMBERT'S STEAK, SEAFOOD AND WHISKEY,
FORT WORTH, DUTCH'S HAMBURGERS, FORT WORTH

As a seventh-generation ranching Texan, Lou Lambert is a consummate West Texan. His grandmother was one of the Old 300: settlers who received land grants in the early 1800s as part of Stephen F. Austin's first colony in Texas. For years, Fort Worth was the edge of the Western Frontier in Texas, but as that line pushed farther and farther west, so did his family, moving out as far as Odessa.

Today, his family maintains cow-calf operations in four west Texas counties. He grew up involved in the 4H club showing calves and working on the family ranch. He went to college in Fort Worth, thinking he'd go into the ranching business with his family, but found he was more drawn to a culinary career.

Working a ranch was an all-day affair, starting well before sunup when a camp cook would have a breakfast going at a campfire. "Our camp cook was Lilo," says Lambert. "He'd have eggs with hot sauce, coffee, and Dutch oven biscuits for us in the morning. Then we'd go work. He'd have made posole or beans or some sort of braised meat for lunch with Dutch oven flatbread. At the end of the day, he'd cook up steaks on a grill over the campfire. It was pretty meat-centric, but you needed it to replenish you from working all day."

As a kid, he remembers when his grandfather would meet people for business at the Inn of the Golden West in Odessa.

"Historically, hotels were the center of the cities in west Texas. That's where business was done; at the white-tablecloth hotel restaurants over lunch. I remember going to the restaurant on the top floor of the Golden West, which was only about seven stories high, and looking out onto the town. To me, I may as well have been looking at New York City from the Empire State Building. It was like being on top of the world. I was enthralled with the formality of it all. The elegance of the dining experience and the food culture around that was fascinating."

Lambert later attended New York's Culinary Institute of America. "I had always wanted to do fine dining, and I thought it had to be in New York, San Francisco, or Chicago," says Lambert who managed to land a job working for up-and-coming Wolfgang Puck in the late 1980s and early '90s.

"I was running his charcuterie department making sausages and smoking and curing meats, and there was this familiarity for me that I couldn't ignore," says Lambert. "In many ways it was the same thing we did back home on the ranch, just in a more formal way. Being away from home made me realize what a rich food culture we really have in Texas."

"Being away from home made me realize what a rich food culture we really have in Texas."

BUTTERMILK BISCUITS

If there's anyone who knows his way around a Dutch oven it's chef Lou Lambert. At his Fort Worth workshop, he has probably more than thirty of them ranging in a variety of sizes that he uses for special events and his own home cooking. The crispy edges the cast-iron oven gives to these little pillows of dough is hard to beat. Try the Dutch oven variation at your next camping outing, or enjoy the traditional oven-baked version any day of the week.

Makes *1 dozen* · **Hands-on** *10 min.* · **Total** *25 min.*

3 cups all-purpose flour
1 Tbsp. baking powder
1 Tbsp. sugar
2 tsp. baking soda
1 tsp. table salt

6 Tbsp. cold butter, cut into pieces
1 ½ cups buttermilk
Parchment paper
1 Tbsp. butter, melted

1. Preheat oven to 450°F. Whisk together first 5 ingredients in a bowl. Cut 6 Tbsp. butter into flour mixture with a pastry blender or fork until crumbly. Add buttermilk, stirring just until dry ingredients are moistened.
2. Turn dough out onto a lightly floured surface, and knead lightly 3 or 4 times. Pat or roll dough to ³/₄-inch thickness; cut with a 2 ¹/₂-inch round cutter, and place ¹/₄ inch apart on a parchment paper-lined baking sheet. Brush with melted butter.
3. Bake at 450°F for 14 to 16 minutes or until golden brown.

CAMPFIRE DUTCH OVEN BUTTERMILK BISCUITS

Prepare recipe as directed in Steps 1 and 2, placing biscuits side by side in a lightly greased 12-inch Dutch oven. Cover with lid, and place 8 hot charcoals beneath oven and 10 to 12 hot charcoals on top of lid. When biscuits begin to rise, reduce bottom coals to 6, and cook until edges of biscuits begin to brown and pull away from side of Dutch oven. Remove Dutch oven from hot coals, and continue cooking with coals on top of lid 15 to 20 minutes or until biscuits are brown and crusty.

TEXAS TOOLS

Dutch Oven

The chuckwagon cook's all-purpose pot and the official Texas State Cooking Implement. This large, deep, and heavy iron skillet with three legs distributes heat evenly and holds it well. It has a heavy lid that makes it a perfect campfire oven for biscuits and cakes, but works just as well as a skillet for steaks, or a pot for making stews, soups, and, of course, chili.

APPLE CAKE COBBLER

Sharing this dessert around a campfire beneath the West Texas stars makes a magical experience delicious. Chef Lou Lambert of Austin shares two methods for his tender apple cake.

Makes *12 servings* · **Hands-on** *20 min.* · **Total** *2 hours*

CRUMB TOPPING
3/4 cup all-purpose flour
1/2 cup granulated sugar
1/4 cup firmly packed brown sugar
1/2 tsp. ground cinnamon
1/4 tsp. table salt
6 Tbsp. cold unsalted butter, cut into
　small pieces
1/4 cup uncooked regular oats

APPLE CAKE COBBLER
1/2 cup unsalted butter
3 lb. apples, peeled and cut into 3/4-inch
　cubes (about 8 cups)

1/2 cup firmly packed brown sugar
2 1/4 cups all-purpose flour
1 1/4 cups granulated sugar
1 Tbsp. baking powder
1 tsp. ground cinnamon
1/2 tsp. table salt
2 1/4 cups milk
1/4 cup buttermilk
2 tsp. vanilla extract

Sweetened whipped cream or vanilla
　ice cream

1. Prepare Crumb Topping: Pulse first 5 ingredients in a food processor until combined. Add butter, and pulse 5 to 7 times or until mixture resembles small peas.
2. Transfer mixture to a small bowl. Stir in oats with a spoon until mixture is crumbly. Chill until ready to use.
3. Prepare Apple Cake Cobbler: Preheat oven to 375°F. Melt butter in a 13- x 9-inch baking dish while oven preheats. Combine apples and brown sugar, tossing to coat. Spoon into baking dish. Bake at 375°F for 15 minutes or until apples begin to soften and release juices.
4. Whisk together flour and next 4 ingredients in a large bowl. Add milk, buttermilk, and vanilla, whisking until smooth. Pour batter over apples in baking dish. Sprinkle with Crumb Topping.
5. Bake at 375°F for 1 hour to 1 hour and 10 minutes or until a wooden pick inserted in center comes out clean. Let stand 15 minutes. Serve warm with whipped cream or ice cream.

CAMPFIRE DUTCH OVEN APPLE CAKE COBBLER

Melt butter in a cast-iron Dutch oven over the fire. Stir in apples and brown sugar. Cook 10 minutes or until apples begin to soften. Pour cobbler batter over apples, and sprinkle with Crumb Topping. Cover with lid, and place 12 hot charcoals on top of lid. Cook 40 to 50 minutes or until a wooden pick inserted in center comes out clean.

MEXICAN WEDDING COOKIES

Mexican wedding cookies are great to make for the holidays. They aren't as sweet as most cookies, even with the addition of the powdered sugar they are rolled in, which makes a nice break from all the other sweet things from the season. For a more festive cookie, divide the dough into two bowls and add green and red food coloring.

Makes *3 ½ dozen* · **Hands-on** *20 min.* · **Total** *2 hours, 10 min.*

1 cup butter, softened
2 ½ cups powdered sugar, divided
2 cups all-purpose flour

½ cup toasted chopped pecans
1 tsp. vanilla extract

1. Beat butter at medium speed with an electric mixer until creamy. Gradually add ½ cup powdered sugar, beating until blended. Add flour to butter mixture, beating at low speed until blended. Stir in pecans and vanilla. Cover dough and chill 1 hour.
2. Preheat oven to 275°F. Shape dough into 42 (1-inch) balls, and place balls 2 inches apart on parchment paper-lined baking sheets. Flatten balls slightly.
3. Bake at 275°F for 30 to 35 minutes or until edges are lightly browned, rotating pans after 15 minutes. Roll hot cookies in remaining 2 cups powdered sugar. Transfer to wire racks, and cool 20 minutes. Reroll cookies in any remaining powdered sugar. Cool cookies completely. Store in an airtight container up to 3 days.

COWBOY COOKIES,
page 249

COWGIRL COOKIES,
page 248

MEXICAN WEDDING
COOKIES,
page 246

COWGIRL COOKIES *(pictured on page 247)*

This chewy cookie was a favorite midday snack served at a dude ranch we visited in the summers during their weekly cowboy lunch cookout. The cookouts followed a horseback trail ride where the ranch wranglers would have an old-fashioned cattle drive cookout waiting for us with these delicious treats for dessert.

Makes *about 5 dozen* · **Hands-on** *20 min.* · **Total** *1 hour, 20 min.*

1 ¹/₂ cups all-purpose flour
¹/₂ tsp. table salt
¹/₂ tsp. baking soda
¹/₂ tsp. ground cinnamon
¹/₄ tsp. freshly grated nutmeg
2 cups firmly packed brown sugar

¹/₂ cup shortening, at room temperature
¹/₂ cup chunky peanut butter
2 large eggs
2 cups uncooked regular oats
1 ¹/₂ cups butterscotch morsels

1. Preheat oven to 375°F. Stir together first 5 ingredients in a large bowl. Beat brown sugar, shortening, and peanut butter at medium speed with an electric mixer until creamy. Add eggs, 1 at a time, beating well after each addition. Beat in 2 Tbsp. water. Gradually add flour mixture, beating at low speed just until blended. Stir in oats and butterscotch morsels.
2. Drop dough using a 1-oz. ice-cream scoop or by 2 tablespoonfuls 3 inches apart onto parchment paper-lined baking sheets. Chill 20 minutes or until firm.
3. Bake at 375°F for 12 to 14 minutes or until edges are golden. Cool on baking sheets 2 minutes; transfer to wire racks, and cool.

COWBOY COOKIES *(pictured on page 247)*

Chocolate chips are a nice flavor contrast for this Cowgirl Cookie sidekick. Make both Cowboy and Cowgirl cookies in smaller portions and bag them up as party favors or hostess gifts.

Makes *about 2 dozen large or 6 dozen small* · **Hands-on** *15 min.* · **Total** *1 hour, 15 min.*

1 cup butter, softened
1 cup granulated sugar
1 cup firmly packed light brown sugar
2 large eggs
1 tsp. vanilla extract
2 ¹/₄ cups all-purpose flour
1 tsp. baking soda

¹/₂ tsp. baking powder
¹/₂ tsp. table salt
2 cups uncooked regular oats
1 (12-oz.) package semisweet chocolate
   morsels (about 2 cups)
1 cup toasted chopped pecans

1. Preheat oven to 350°F. Beat butter at medium speed with an electric mixer until creamy. Gradually add sugars, beating at medium speed until mixture is light and fluffy. Add eggs, 1 at a time, beating well after each addition. Beat in vanilla.
2. Combine flour and next 3 ingredients. Stir in oats. Gradually add flour mixture to sugar mixture, beating at low speed just until blended. Stir in chocolate morsels and nuts.
3. Drop dough using a 2-oz. ice-cream scoop or by one-fourth cupfuls 3 inches apart onto parchment paper-lined baking sheets. Chill 20 minutes or until firm.
4. Bake at 350°F for 16 to 18 minutes or until cookies are set, rotating pans after 12 minutes. Cool on pans 2 minutes; transfer to wire racks, and cool.

Note: For smaller cookies, use a 1-oz. scoop or drop by 2 tablespoonfuls, and decrease bake time to 12 to 14 minutes.

TEXAS TIDBIT

MARFA LIGHTS

Considering the effect time in the desert can have on people, it's not unusual to come to the conclusion that the storied Marfa Lights may just be a figment of the imagination—or even a drug-induced hallucination. But when you consider the great many accounts of this strange phenomenon recorded since the 19th century, it's hard to refute the notion that they actually exist. Sometimes red, blue, and white, the mysterious lights appear randomly throughout the night regardless of the season or the weather. The official Marfa Lights Viewing Area is nine miles east of Marfa on Highway 90.

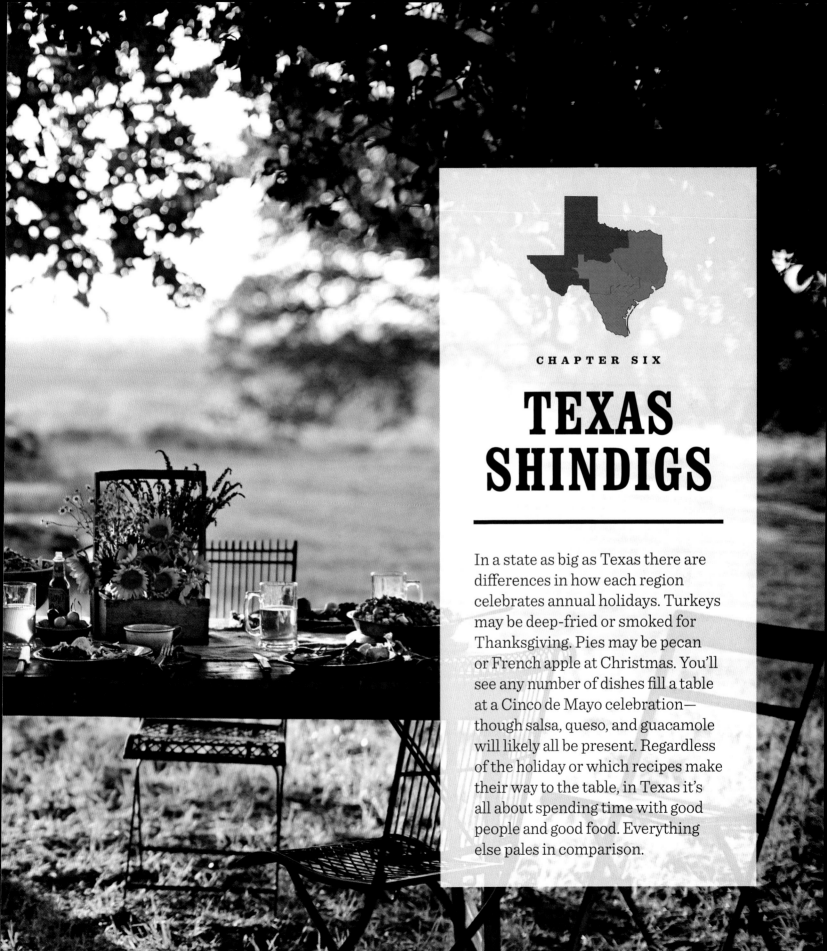

CHAPTER SIX

TEXAS SHINDIGS

In a state as big as Texas there are differences in how each region celebrates annual holidays. Turkeys may be deep-fried or smoked for Thanksgiving. Pies may be pecan or French apple at Christmas. You'll see any number of dishes fill a table at a Cinco de Mayo celebration—though salsa, queso, and guacamole will likely all be present. Regardless of the holiday or which recipes make their way to the table, in Texas it's all about spending time with good people and good food. Everything else pales in comparison.

CLASSIC
MARGARITA,
page 255

TEXAS BEEFED-UP
BLOODY MARY,
page 257

THE RIO STAR,
page 254

MICHELADA,
page 256

HERMAN MARSHALL
SIDECAR,
page 255

COCKTAILS

Texas cocktails are bold, rustic, and often come with a kick. After Prohibition, the state's cocktails relied on spirits produced elsewhere. But since 1997, when Tito Beveridge won the state's first distilling permit post-Prohibition, distilleries have boomed. These days Texas cocktails made with native spirits are mixology made in Lone Star heaven.

HYE BALL,
page 254

SANGRIA BLANCO,
page 256

RANCH RUNNER PUNCH,
page 257

HYE BALL

Hye, Texas, winery William Chris Vineyards uses their own fortified Roussanne white wine in this variation on a classic. They aptly named their refreshing summer beverage a Hye Ball.

Makes *1 serving* · **Hands-on** *10 min.* · **Total** *10 min.*

1 tsp. fresh lemon juice
3 to 4 fresh mint leaves
2 ½ Tbsp. sweet white wine

2 ½ Tbsp. vodka
¼ cup tonic water
Garnishes: fresh mint sprig, lemon slices

Muddle first 2 ingredients in a cocktail shaker. Add wine, vodka, and ice. Cover with lid, and shake vigorously until thoroughly chilled (about 30 seconds). Strain mixture into a Collins glass filled with ice; top with tonic water. Serve immediately.

Note: We tested with Sauternes for sweet white wine. You may also use white port.

THE RIO STAR

Rio Star grapefruit are one of the state's most prized agricultural creations. The juice is both tart and sweet and offers a bright lingering finish. And mixed with a little vodka and elderflower liqueur makes the Texas grapefruit a star of a whole different caliber. Though this citrus fruit is in season during the winter, this cocktail is a sensation during the summer.

Makes *1 serving* · **Hands-on** *10 min.* · **Total** *10 min.*

¼ cup vodka
2 Tbsp. fresh red grapefruit juice
1 ½ Tbsp. elderflower liqueur

3 Tbsp. sparkling wine
Garnish: grapefruit slice

Combine first 3 ingredients in a cocktail shaker; fill with ice. Cover with lid, and shake vigorously until thoroughly chilled (about 30 seconds). Strain vodka mixture into a chilled cocktail glass; top with sparkling wine.

Note: We tested with Tito's vodka and St-Germain elderflower liqueur.

HERMAN MARSHALL SIDECAR

A classic from the 1850s, the Sidecar balances sweet and tart in one smooth drink. While typically made with Cognac, it's always fun to play around with different base spirits. This spin on the Sidecar was created by my friend David Toby of Jack Allen's Kitchen using rye whiskey from Texas' Herman Marshall Distillery.

Makes *1 serving* · **Hands-on** *10 min.* · **Total** *10 min.*

¼ cup rye whiskey
1 Tbsp. orange liqueur
1 Tbsp. Round Rock Honey-Fig Syrup

1 ½ tsp. fresh lemon juice
Garnishes: fresh or dried fig half, orange twist

Combine all ingredients except garnishes in a large cocktail shaker; fill with ice, if desired. Cover with lid, and shake vigorously until thoroughly chilled (about 30 seconds). Strain whiskey mixture into a cocktail glass filled with ice, if desired. Serve immediately.

Note: We tested with Herman Marshall Texas Rye Whiskey and Paula's Texas Orange Liqueur.

CLASSIC MARGARITA

A classic margarita mixes good tequila, lime, and orange liqueur. But as one of the country's most consumed cocktails, the little "Mexican Daisy" has endured constant evolution—a few are good, most are bad. If it sticks close to the three simple ingredients listed above, using a 100% blue agave tequila, you're in the right ballpark. If it resembles a Slurpee and comes in a glowing Soylent green color, run fast.

Makes *4 servings* · **Hands-on** *5 min.* · **Total** *5 min.*

1 cup 100% blue agave silver tequila
½ cup orange liqueur
¼ cup Basic Simple Syrup

½ cup fresh lime juice (about 6 medium limes)
Garnish: lime slices

Stir together tequila, orange liqueur, ¼ cup Basic Simple Syrup, and lime juice in a large pitcher. Fill cocktail shaker with ice cubes; pour desired amount of mixture into cocktail shaker. Cover with lid, and shake vigorously until thoroughly chilled (about 30 seconds). Strain into chilled glasses with salted rims. Serve immediately.

Round Rock Honey-Fig Syrup

Bring 1 cup water to a boil in a small saucepan over medium-high heat. Reduce heat to medium-low. Stir in ¼ cup honey and 4 dried sliced figs, and simmer 15 minutes or until figs are rehydrated and tender. Pour through a fine wire-mesh strainer into a bowl; discard solids. Cool completely. Refrigerate in an airtight container up to 2 weeks. **Makes** *1 cup*

Basic Simple Syrup

Combine ¼ cup sugar and ¼ cup water in a 1-cup glass measuring cup; microwave at HIGH 1 ½ minutes or until mixture boils. Stir until sugar dissolves. Cool to room temperature (about 30 minutes). Refrigerate in an airtight container up to 1 month. **Makes** *⅓ cup*

MICHELADA

Recipes for the Michelada abound. A poll of of friends in Mexico City was unanimous: ice cold cerveza with salt and limon (lime). Everything else is a departure from the real deal. Ask for Michelada con Clamato if you want tomato flavor. In other parts of Mexico, a Michelada may come with tomato juice and assorted spices so if you want the straightforward classic, ask for a "Suero."

Makes *1 serving* · **Hands-on** *5 min.* · **Total** *5 min.*

2 Tbsp. fresh lime juice
2 tsp. Mexican hot sauce
Dash of Worcestershire sauce

Pinch of celery salt
1 (12-oz.) bottle chilled Mexican beer
Garnish: lime slices

Stir together lime juice, and next 3 ingredients in a chilled beer glass with a salted rim. Slowly add beer, and stir gently just until blended.

Note: We tested with Pacifico beer and Cholula hot sauce.

SANGRIA BLANCO

Many people whip up red sangria, but I've found this sparkling white version to be a big hit. Substitute fresh peaches for the strawberries to change things up. You'll find a pitcher of these goes pretty fast.

Makes *10 servings* · **Hands-on** *20 min.* · **Total** *1 hour, 20 min.*

2 oranges, thinly sliced
2 lemons, thinly sliced
2 limes, thinly sliced
²/₃ cup sugar
1 ¹/₄ cups white tequila

1 (750-ml.) bottle chilled dry white wine
1 (750-ml.) bottle chilled dry sparkling wine
3 ¹/₃ cups quartered fresh strawberries
Garnsh: mint or basil sprigs

Combine first 4 ingredients in a large pitcher; pour tequila over fruit mixture, and let stand for 1 hour, stirring every 15 minutes. Stir in white wine, sparkling wine, and strawberries. Serve immediately over ice.

RANCH RUNNER PUNCH

In the islands, Rum Runners have a reputation for fostering a festive environment, and in Texas it's no different. This particular twist uses watermelon, a ubiquitous summer roadside stand staple.

Makes *11 cups* · **Hands-on** *20 min.* · **Total** *20 min.*

1 (12-lb.) seedless watermelon, cut into
    chunks
2 cups light rum
1 cup firmly packed light brown sugar

1 cup fresh lemon juice (about 5 lemons)
¹/₂ cup fresh lime juice (about 5 limes)
Garnishes: lime slices, mint sprigs, and
    watermelon slices

1. Process watermelon in a blender or food processor until smooth. Pour through a fine wire-mesh strainer into a large pitcher or punch bowl, using back of a spoon to squeeze out juice; discard solids.
2. Stir rum and next 3 ingredients into juice. Serve over ice.

Note: We tested with Treaty Oak Rum.

TEXAS BEEFED-UP BLOODY MARY

My step-grandmother, Deane Rowe, made Bloody Marys with "Beefamato," a beefed-up version of Clamato that's hard to find. Add beef broth for similar results. Without it, a truly Texas version of this all-American cocktail is all hat and no cattle.

Makes *4 servings* · **Hands-on** *20 min.* · **Total** *20 min.*

2 cups tomato juice
1 cup vodka
³/₄ cup beef broth
¹/₄ cup fresh lime juice (about 2 limes)
2 tsp. prepared horseradish

4 tsp. Worcestershire sauce
1 tsp. hot sauce
³/₄ tsp. celery salt
Garnishes: celery, green olives

Stir together first 8 ingredients in a cocktail shaker. Fill with ice cubes. Cover with lid, and shake vigorously until thoroughly chilled (about 30 seconds). Strain into glasses filled with ice.

Note: We tested with Tito's vodka and Tabasco red hot sauce.

METRIC EQUIVALENTS

The recipes that appear in this cookbook use the standard United States method for measuring liquid and dry or solid ingredients (teaspoons, tablespoons, and cups). The information in the following charts is provided to help cooks outside the U.S. successfully use these recipes. All equivalents are approximate.

Metric Equivalents for Different Types of Ingredients

A standard cup measure of a dry or solid ingredient will vary in weight depending on the type of ingredient. A standard cup of liquid is the same volume for any type of liquid. Use the following chart when converting standard cup measures to grams (weight) or milliliters (volume).

Standard Cup	Fine Powder (ex. flour)	Grain (ex. rice)	Granular (ex. sugar)	Liquid Solids (ex. butter)	Liquid (ex. milk)
1	140 g	150 g	190 g	200 g	240 ml
3/4	105 g	113 g	143 g	150 g	180 ml
2/3	93 g	100 g	125 g	133 g	160 ml
1/2	70 g	75 g	95 g	100 g	120 ml
1/3	47 g	50 g	63 g	67 g	80 ml
1/4	35 g	38 g	48 g	50 g	60 ml
1/8	18 g	19 g	24 g	25 g	30 ml

Useful Equivalents for Liquid Ingredients by Volume

1/4 tsp					=	1 ml		
1/2 tsp					=	2 ml		
1 tsp					=	5 ml		
3 tsp	=	1 Tbsp			=	1/2 fl oz	=	15 ml
		2 Tbsp	=	1/8 cup	=	1 fl oz	=	30 ml
		4 Tbsp	=	1/4 cup	=	2 fl oz	=	60 ml
		5 1/3 Tbsp	=	1/3 cup	=	3 fl oz	=	80 ml
		8 Tbsp	=	1/2 cup	=	4 fl oz	=	120 ml
		10 2/3 Tbsp	=	2/3 cup	=	5 fl oz	=	160 ml
		12 Tbsp	=	3/4 cup	=	6 fl oz	=	180 ml
		16 Tbsp	=	1 cup	=	8 fl oz	=	240 ml
		1 pt	=	2 cups	=	16 fl oz	=	480 ml
		1 qt	=	4 cups	=	32 fl oz	=	960 ml
						33 fl oz	=	1000 ml = 1 l

Useful Equivalents for Dry Ingredients by Weight

(To convert ounces to grams, multiply the number of ounces by 30.)

1 oz	=	1/16 lb	=	30 g
4 oz	=	1/4 lb	=	120 g
8 oz	=	1/2 lb	=	240 g
12 oz	=	3/4 lb	=	360 g
16 oz	=	1 lb	=	480 g

Useful Equivalents for Length

(To convert inches to centimeters, multiply the number of inches by 2.5.)

1 in			=	2.5 cm		
6 in	=	1/2 ft	=	15 cm		
12 in	=	1 ft	=	30 cm		
36 in	=	3 ft	= 1 yd	90 cm		
40 in			=	100 cm	=	1 m

Useful Equivalents for Cooking/Oven Temperatures

	Fahrenheit	Celsius	Gas Mark
Freeze Water	32° F	0° C	
Room Temperature	68° F	20° C	
Boil Water	212° F	100° C	
Bake	325° F	160° C	3
	350° F	180° C	4
	375° F	190° C	5
	400° F	200° C	6
	425° F	220° C	7
	450° F	230° C	8
Broil			Grill

SUBJECT INDEX

RECEIPE INDEX

PHOTO CREDITS

SL Allison (iStock): 44-45; Kenny Braun: 9, 102–103, 116–117, 130–131, 142–143, 158, 188;
Robbie Caponetto (*Southern Living*): 110; Jody Horton: 16, 22, 32, 68; Wyatt McSpadden: 214, 224;
Art Meripol (*Southern Living*): 202–203; Pamela Moore (Getty): 52–53; Gustav Schmiege III: 240;
Gregor Schuster (Getty): 17, 33, 69, 83, 111, 125, 159, 189, 225, 241; Yeben Wu (Getty): 4-5

ABOUT THE AUTHOR

Jessica Dupuy is a native Texan who writes about wine, spirits, food, and travel. She is a contributing wine and spirits columnist for *Texas Monthly* magazine and has regular credits for *Imbibe* magazine, Wine Review Online, and Fodor's travel publications.

Her magazine work has also been featured in *National Geographic Traveler, The Hollywood Reporter, Texas Highways,* and numerous Austin publications.

She has also written *Uchi: The Cookbook,* in conjunction with James Beard Award-winning Executive Chef Tyson Cole; *The Salt Lick Cookbook: A Story of Land, Family and Love* on the iconic Texas barbecue restaurant; and the *Jack Allen's Kitchen Cookbook* about revealing the true flavors of Texas through its seasons and farming community.

Dupuy holds a BA in History from Trinity University and a MA in Journalism from the Medill School of Journalism at Northwestern University. She is a member of Les Dames D'Escoffier–Austin and on the Advisory board for the Wine and Food Foundation of Texas. She lives in Austin and enjoys cooking with her kids, Gus and Ashlyn, sharing great wine with friends, and fly-fishing with her husband, Myers.

A NOTE OF THANKS...

Thank you to God and Texas and for the blessing of being a native daughter.

A special thank you to my mom for letting me sit on the kitchen counter next to you as a little girl while you baked. To my dad for mastering the grill with all manner of meats—and for using tarragon as your secret ingredient. To my grandmothers, Joyce and Marian, and to Aunt Jamie, Aunt Dana, Aunt Susan, Uncle Craig, Robin, Jamie, Craig, Joy, Zoe, Lauren, Martha, Fritzi, and Julie for making meals that will last our family generations. To my brother, Jake, for being the best sidekick growing up. To Marilu for loving on my kids while I was cooking and writing.

Thanks to my dad, Dr. Char Miller, Larry McMurtry, Pat Sharpe, Courtney Bond, Sam Gwynne, Tyson Cole, Morgan Weber, Daniel Vaughn, Robb Walsh, Lou Lambert, Tom Perini, Stephan Pyles, Tim Byres, Jesse Griffiths, Andrew Wiseheart, Johnny Hernandez, Melissa Guerra, Chris Shepherd, Jack Gilmore, and Scott Roberts for giving me a deep and profound love for Texas, its history, and the food that defines its identity.

Most important, to Myers, Gus, and Ashlyn: I love you.

A NOTE FROM THE EDITOR:

Special thanks to Margie and Don Reynolds, the entire extended Reynolds family, and everyone at Squaw Creek Ranch for hosting the team from Oxmoor House and enabling us to get such beautiful location photos. Hats off to Noe, Nosito, and Max Arroyos, Reynolds Harvey, Ben Williams, Jerry Baird, J.D. Barham, Jennifer Miller, Cindy Cook, Shelbie and Sam Gaddy, Sally Jo Barham, Shari Guthrey, Misty Cook, and Colt Rhodes.